CARING FOR PEOPLE

COMMUNITY CARE IN THE NEXT DECADE AND BEYOND

Presented to Parliament by the Secretaries of State
for Health, Social Security, Wales
and Scotland by Command of Her Majesty
November 1989.

LONDON : HMSO

Cm 849

£10.00 net

Caring for People : Community Care in the Next Decade and Beyond

Foreword

Helping people to lead, as far as is possible, full and independent lives is at the heart of the Government's approach to community care. Improving the services that enable them to do that is a continuing commitment shared by all concerned.

There is a great deal to be proud of in the progress that has been achieved. The greater part of care has been, is and always will be provided by families and friends. At the same time dedicated staff working in local authorities, the health service and the independent sector have all made a contribution to the many innovative and successful schemes in existence.

We believe that the proposals in the White Paper provide a coherent framework to meet present and future challenges. They will give people a much better opportunity to secure the services they need and will stimulate public agencies to tailor services to individuals' needs. This offers the prospect of a better deal for people who need care and for those who provide care. Our aim is to promote choice as well as independence.

Building on the valuable work done by Sir Roy Griffiths, the White Paper expands the statement which the Secretary of State for Health made on behalf of the Government in July, for example on the way in which assessment of individuals' needs will work. We have benefitted from discussion and consultation with leading organisations and individuals working in the community care field, and this will continue as we take the necessary further steps towards implementation, and the formal guidance that is proposed.

This White Paper heralds a period of intense activity in order to plan and prepare for the implementation of the changes we propose. For those in local government in particular the challenge is to create the conditions in which the new arrangements may flourish and produce real benefit. We shall play our part in securing the necessary changes. To achieve success, local government, the National Health Service and the independent sectors must work in an effective partnership and pay close attention to the views of those in need of help.

We do not underestimate the size and importance of the task facing us all. We believe that our proposals offer a great opportunity to strengthen our caring services for the 1990s and beyond for the benefit of those most in need.

Secretary of State for Health

Secretary of State for Social Security

Secretary of State for Wales

Secretary of State for Scotland

Contents

Olive Campbell

CHAPTER ONE: BETTER COMMUNITY CARE SERVICES

CHAPTER ONE: BETTER COMMUNITY CARE SERVICES

The Government's Commitment to Community Care

1.1 Community care means providing the services and support which people who are affected by problems of ageing, mental illness, mental handicap or physical or sensory disability need to be able to live as independently as possible in their own homes, or in "homely" settings in the community. The Government is firmly committed to a policy of community care which enables such people to achieve their full potential.

1.2 This White Paper sets out the Government's proposals for improving community care. It complements the proposals in the White Paper "Working for Patients" (CM555) for the management of the hospital and family practitioner services. Taken together, the two White Papers set out how the Government believes health and social care services should develop over the next decade.

1.3 The Government is pursuing separately in the Children Bill, at present before Parliament, a major reform of children's services in England and Wales to be implemented in 1991. The two programmes are consistent and complementary and, taken together, set a fresh agenda and new challenges for social services authorities for the next decade. There is no intention of creating a division between child care and community care services; the full range of social services authority functions should continue to form a coherent whole.

The Government's Record

1.4 The successful implementation of community care policy depends crucially on the availability of, and ease of access to, adequate and appropriate services in the community. The past decade has been one of substantial growth in community care services, made possible by a significant increase in expenditure by central and local government.

1.5 The Government's commitment to investing in community care is set out in some detail in Chapter 8. The following key achievements can be highlighted:

- gross current expenditure on core community care services has risen from £1,169m in 1979/80 to £3,444m in 1987/88 - a real terms increase of 68%;
- local authority personal social services net expenditure has grown by 37% in real terms during the decade up to 1989/90, while expenditure on community health services has grown by 35% in real terms up to 1987/88;
- social security support for people in independent residential care and nursing homes rose from £10m in 1979 to over £1,000m in May 1989;
- between 1979/80 and 1987/88, the number of places in local authority and registered residential homes rose by 47% to 302,600 while local authority home help staff increased by 27%;

- the number of places in residential homes and NHS community units for people with a mental handicap rose by 13,900 to 29,700 between 1979/80 and 1986/87.

The Need For Change

1.6 Progress has, however, been slower and less even than the Government would like, and the arrangements for public funding have contained a built-in bias towards residential and nursing home care, rather than services for people at home. While some areas have made great strides in the development of community services, others are less well advanced. The Government's intention is that in future authorities should be given better opportunities to achieve consistent performance in line with people's needs.

1.7 The focus of this White Paper is on clarifying roles and responsibilities, bringing together the relevant sources of finance, delegating responsibility for decision making to the local level wherever possible, improving accountability and providing the right incentives. The Government is seeking to establish the right financial and managerial framework which will help to secure the delivery of good quality local services in line with national policy objectives.

The Government's Approach To Achieving Better Care

1.8 The Government believes that for most people community care offers the best form of care available - certainly with better quality and choice than they might have expected in the past. The changes outlined in this White Paper are intended to:

- enable people to live as normal a life as possible in their own homes or in a homely environment in the local community;
- provide the right amount of care and support to help people achieve maximum possible independence and, by acquiring or reacquiring basic living skills, help them to achieve their full potential;
- give people a greater individual say in how they live their lives and the services they need to help them to do so.

Promoting choice and independence underlies all the Government's proposals.

1.9 The Government acknowledges that the great bulk of community care is provided by friends, family and neighbours. The decision to take on a caring role is never an easy one. However, many people make that choice and it is right that they should be able to play their part in looking after those close to them. But it must be recognised that carers need help and support if they are to continue to carry out their role; and many people will not have carers readily available who can meet all their needs.

1.10 The Government therefore believes that the key components of community care should be:

- services that respond flexibly and sensitively to the needs of individuals and their carers;
- services that allow a range of options for consumers;
- services that intervene no more than is necessary to foster independence;
- services that concentrate on those with the greatest needs.

Key Objectives

1.11 The Government's proposals have six key objectives for service delivery:

- ***to promote the development of domiciliary, day and respite services to enable people to live in their own homes wherever feasible and sensible.*** Existing funding structures have worked against the development of such services. In future, the Government will encourage the targeting of home-based services on those people whose need for them is greatest.
- ***to ensure that service providers make practical support for carers a high priority.*** Assessment of care needs should always take account of the needs of caring family, friends and neighbours;
- ***to make proper assessment of need and good case management the cornerstone of high quality care.*** Packages of care should then be designed in line with individual needs and preferences;
- ***to promote the development of a flourishing independent sector alongside good quality public services.*** The Government has endorsed Sir Roy Griffiths' recommendation that social services authorities should be "enabling" agencies. It will be their responsibility to make maximum possible use of private and voluntary providers, and so increase the available range of options and widen consumer choice;
- ***to clarify the responsibilities of agencies and so make it easier to hold them to account for their performance.*** The Government recognises that the present confusion has contributed to poor overall performance;
- ***to secure better value for taxpayers' money by introducing a new funding structure for social care.*** The Government's aim is that social security provisions should not, as they do now, provide any incentive in favour of residential and nursing home care.

Key Changes

1.12 In order to achieve these objectives, the Government proposes to make a number of changes in the way in which social care is delivered and funded:

First, local authorities are to become responsible, in collaboration with medical, nursing and other interests, for assessing individual need, designing care arrangements and securing their delivery within available resources;

second, local authorities will be expected to produce and publish clear plans for the development of community care services, consistent with the plans of health authorities and other interested agencies. The Government will take new powers to ensure that plans are open to inspection, and to call for reports from social services authorities;

third, local authorities will be expected to make maximum use of the independent sector. The Government will ensure that they have acceptable plans for achieving this;

fourth, there will be a new funding structure for those seeking public support for residential and nursing home care from April 1991. After that date local authorities will take responsibility for financial support of people in private and voluntary homes, over and above any general social security entitlements. The new arrangements will not, however, apply to people already resident in homes before April 1991;

fifth, applicants with few or no resources of their own will be eligible for the same levels of Income Support and Housing Benefit, irrespective of whether they are living in their own homes or in independent residential or nursing homes;

sixth, local authorities will be required to establish inspection and registration units at arm's length from the management of their own services which will be responsible for checking on standards in both their own homes and in independent sector residential care homes;

seventh, there will be a new specific grant to promote the development of social care for seriously mentally ill people.

Scope of Proposals

1.13 For the most part, the proposals in this White Paper will apply equally to England, Wales and Scotland, although some will need to be adapted to the particular circumstances of the health and social services in Wales and Scotland. Chapters 1-8 are written in terms which apply primarily to England, Chapter 9 relates to the position in Great Britain as a whole. Chapters 10 and 11 look specifically at the approach to be taken in Scotland and Wales.

1.14 Northern Ireland has its own distinctive structure for the management of health and social services. The Government plans to publish a separate policy paper for Northern Ireland shortly.

CHAPTER TWO: COMMUNITY CARE IN PRACTICE

CHAPTER TWO: COMMUNITY CARE IN PRACTICE

2.1 Enabling people to live as independently as possible in the community is at the heart of community care. To do so, people frequently need both social care and health care. The Government's primary focus in this White Paper is on the reform of the organisation and funding of social care. The responsibilities of the health service are essentially unaltered, and the health care contribution to community care remains of fundamental importance. The emphasis in the NHS will continue to be to support people in the community, through the general practitioner and community health services, wherever and whenever that is practical. Improved social care should make it possible in a greater number of cases.

What Is Community Care?

2.2 Community care means providing the right level of intervention and support to enable people to achieve maximum independence and control over their own lives. For this aim to become a reality, the development of a wide range of services provided in a variety of settings is essential. These services form part of a spectrum of care, ranging from domiciliary support provided to people in their own homes, strengthened by the availability of respite care and day care for those with more intensive care needs, through sheltered housing, group homes and hostels where increasing levels of care are available, to residential care and nursing homes and long-stay hospital care for those for whom other forms of care are no longer enough.

The Contribution of Carers

2.3 While this White Paper focuses largely on the role of statutory and independent bodies in the provision of community care services, the reality is that most care is provided by family, friends and neighbours. The majority of carers take on these responsibilities willingly, but the Government recognises that many need help to be able to manage what can become a heavy burden. Their lives can be made much easier if the right support is there at the right time, and a key responsibility of statutory service providers should be to do all they can to assist and support carers. Helping carers to maintain their valuable contribution to the spectrum of care is both right and a sound investment. Help may take the form of providing advice and support as well as practical services such as day, domiciliary and respite care.

Social Care

2.4 Social care and practical assistance with daily living are key components of good quality community care. The services and facilities, at present largely the responsibility of social services authorities, which will be essential to enable people to live in the community include help with personal and domestic tasks such as cleaning, washing and preparing meals, with disablement equipment and home adaptations, transport, budgeting and other aspects of daily living. Suitable good quality housing is essential and the availability of day care, respite care, leisure facilities and employment and educational opportunities will all improve the quality of life enjoyed by a person with care needs.

2.5 The Government recognises that some people will continue to need residential or nursing home care. For such people, this form of care should be a positive choice. And there will be others, in particular elderly and seriously mentally ill people and some people with serious mental handicaps together with other illnesses or disabilities, whose combination of health and social care needs is best met by care in a hospital setting. There will be a continuing need for this form of care.

Health Care

2.6 Medical and nursing care can be of equal importance to social care. The primary health care team has a vital role to play: in many cases, the GP will be the first port of call for people in the community, and will continue to meet most of their basic health care needs. Community nurses who, for the purpose of this document, include district nurses, health visitors, community psychiatric nurses and mental handicap nurses, are often in the most regular contact with patients and have a very significant role to play. And the skills and contribution of therapists, other health care professionals and secondary health care services will continue to be very valuable.

Social Security

2.7 The Government will continue to provide a system of financial support for those who need care and for their carers. The social security system provides financial support in a number of ways: through Invalid Care Allowance, through disability benefits, and through Income Support, Housing Benefit and the Social Fund. The scale of expenditure on these benefits reflects both the numbers needing support, and the Government's commitment to supporting them. Expenditure as a whole on carers and on the disabled has risen from £1,759m in 1979 to £7,290m today, an increase of 89% in real terms. These figures demonstrate the Government's commitment to a fair and flexible system of support .

Who Needs Community Care?

2.8 Many people need some extra help and support at some stage in their lives, as a result of illness or temporary disability. Some people, as a result of the effects of old age, of mental illness including dementia, of mental handicap or physical disability or sensory impairment, have a continuing need for care on a longer-term basis. People with drug and alcohol related disorders, people with multiple handicaps and people with progressive illnesses such as AIDS or multiple sclerosis may also need community care at some time.

People from Ethnic Minorities

2.9 The Government recognises that people from different cultural backgrounds may have particular care needs and problems. Minority communities may have different concepts of community care and it is important that service providers are sensitive to these variations. Good community care will take account of the circumstances of minority communities and will be planned in consultation with them.

Responding to Different Needs

2.10 Most of this White Paper is about the general mechanisms through which community care ought to be delivered, regardless of varying needs, but the Government recognises that there are significant variations in need between different groups of people. For the most vulnerable groups, that is those affected by the problems of ageing and/or by physical, mental or sensory disability, the Government wishes to promote particular priorities and to develop community care in the light of them.

Priorities for Elderly and Disabled People

2.11 The recent OPCS disability surveys have suggested that over six million adults of all ages have some physical, mental or sensory disability ranging from very slight to severe. The majority (over 4m) are over 65. Most people over 65 are active, energetic and independent citizens. Nearly all want to be a part of the community, in their own homes. Some have a variety of needs for help and support, a large amount of which is willingly and ably provided by relatives, friends and neighbours, and the activities of the voluntary and charitable sectors. Younger disabled people, particularly those in the period of transition from youth to adulthood, have special needs in terms of establishing relationships, securing employment and achieving an active role in society alongside their counterparts.

2.12 The policy of successive Governments has been to promote community based services which encourage and prolong independent living. The Government sees the development of community care as set out in this White Paper as a reinforcement of this objective. It places particular emphasis on the following priorities:

First, promoting positive and healthy lifestyles among all age groups through health education and the development of effective health surveillance and screening programmes and so reducing as far as possible the need for in-patient and residential care;

second, promoting through planning agreements between health authorities, primary care services, local authorities and the independent sector, coherent networks of local services designed to encourage and assist people to live dignified and independent lives in their own homes;

third, providing for those who require it a full range of facilities which would include acute hospital in-patient services, continuing health care provision including specialist departments of geriatric medicine, and therapy services as well as the full range of social services;

fourth, avoiding unnecessary institutional care by ensuring that decisions on the provision of services are made on the basis of a careful assessment of need;

fifth, ensuring improved access to information about local and national facilities including respite care, and a greater involvement of patients, clients and carers in the development of services.

Priorities for People with a Mental Handicap

2.13 The majority of people with a mental handicap have always lived in the community, although only twenty five years ago almost 60,000 lived in specialist mental handicap hospitals, sometimes of a thousand or more beds.

2.14 Over the eighteen years since the White Paper "Better Services for the Mentally Handicapped" it has become increasingly recognised that the needs of the most handicapped people, even those whose handicap is severe, are largely for social, rather than health, care. Increasingly, therefore, services are taking the form of packages of social care for people living independently, or supported in small group homes or residential communities. As a consequence, the numbers in specialist mental handicap hospitals have reduced steadily to the present level of around 30,000. This progress is due to the energy and creativity which staff of all disciplines in the health and social services and the voluntary sector have shown in developing new forms of service.

2.15 The Government wishes to promote further progress within available resources and is exploring how this can best be done. In particular, it wishes to encourage the provision of services to individuals, developed from a multi-disciplinary assessment of their needs and made with proper participation of the individuals concerned, their families and other carers.

2.16 When these new forms of service are sufficiently developed, people with a mental handicap should only be in NHS facilities when they have medical or nursing needs which cannot practicably be met other than in such facilities. There will be an increasing need for an appropriate range of health care to be available, both through general and hospital practice, domiciliary services and, as necessary, specialist services. There will continue to be an important role for those such as consultants in the psychiatry of mental handicap with particular knowledge and experience of treating patients with a mental handicap.

2.17 The mental handicap nursing profession plays a particularly important role in providing treatment, care and support to people with a mental handicap, both in hospital and in a range of community settings. Nurses' skills and experience are highly valued and will continue to be needed as part of the new forms of service which will be increasingly the responsibility of local authorities. The Department of Health will be exploring with the professions, the Local Authority Associations, and other interests how this can best be facilitated.

2.18 The objective since 1981 that no child requiring long term residential care should grow up in a mental handicap hospital has been very largely achieved through the development of new provision. Ministers wish to see the objective wholly achieved within a reasonable timescale.

Priorities for Mentally Ill People

2.19 The Government recognises that the implementation of community care for people with a mental illness has given rise to particular concerns. Objectives for this group, and specific proposals to improve matters, are set out in Chapter 7.

Working Together

2.20 As has been recognised in child care, it is essential that the caring services should work effectively together, each recognising and respecting the others' contribution and responsibilities. Much of this White Paper is about the clarification of those responsibilities. Nonetheless, it will continue to be essential for each of the relevant services to keep in mind the interests and responsibilities of the other; to recognise that particularly at the working interface there is frequently much common purpose; to cross-refer cases when appropriate; and to seek and share advice and information when relevant. There is no room in community care for a narrow view of individuals' needs, nor of ways of meeting them.

2.21 Nor should community care be seen as the prerogative of public services. People like to take responsibility for their own needs wherever possible. We are fortunate in having a thriving voluntary sector, and a rapidly growing private sector. The Government believes that people welcome this mixed provision of care, and that it encourages innovation, diversity, proper attention to quality and the interests of consumers. The rest of this White Paper is about how care should be better organised and managed for the benefit of the people who need it.

CHAPTER THREE: ROLES AND RESPONSIBILITIES OF SOCIAL SERVICES AUTHORITIES

CHAPTER THREE: ROLES AND RESPONSIBILITIES OF SOCIAL SERVICES AUTHORITIES

3.1 INTRODUCTION

3.1.1 Social services authorities already have a wide range of statutory powers and duties to help vulnerable people in the community. They are responsible for meeting social care needs in their areas by arranging the provision of residential, day and domiciliary care services and respite care. They are able to charge for such services, taking account of clients' ability to pay. The proposals in this White Paper build on those responsibilities.

3.1.2 In 1987/88 local authorities in England spent £2,350m on community care: £1,183m on residential care and £1,167m on domiciliary and day care services. Social Services Departments employed 232,000 staff in total : 5,500 managers, 27,000 social work staff, 1,100 occupational therapists, 88,200 staff in residential care establishments, 59,500 home help service staff and 27,200 staff in day care establishments. The volume of services provided was also large:

- 133,800 places in local authority residential care homes;
- 46.4 million meals on wheels; and
- 108,700 places in day centres.

Chapter 8 illustrates the expansion in volume of these services over the past decade.

3.1.3 Although local authorities are responsible for providing residential care for those who need it, an increasing share of that responsibility has in recent years been carried by the rapidly expanding private provision of such care, much of it funded through the availability of social security allowances for people in residential care homes. While welcoming that extension of choice, the Government accepts the view of Sir Roy Griffiths and others that the provision of care at public expense should be preceded by a proper assessment of the individual's needs, and in particular whether they could be met while enabling the individual to continue to live independently. The Government also endorses Sir Roy's vision of authorities as arrangers and purchasers of care services rather than as monopolistic providers. In future, social services departments will have the following key responsibilities:

- carrying out an appropriate assessment of an individual's need for social care (including residential and nursing home care), in collaboration as necessary with medical, nursing and other caring agencies, before deciding what services should be provided;
- designing packages of services tailored to meet the assessed needs of individuals and their carers. The appointment of a "case manager" may facilitate this;
- securing the delivery of services, not simply by acting as direct providers, but by developing their purchasing and contracting role to become "enabling authorities";

- establishing procedures for receiving comments and complaints from service users;
- monitoring the quality and cost-effectiveness of services, with medical and nursing advice as appropriate;
- establishing arrangements for assessing the client's ability to contribute to the full economic cost to the local authority of residential services.

3.1.4 All social services authorities will be expected to discharge these responsibilities effectively and efficiently. In order to do so, authorities may need to strengthen their existing management arrangements. In particular, they will need to give attention to the adequacy of systems for planning, accountability, financial control, purchasing and quality control. Support services, like training for staff at all levels, will also need early attention. The aim should be to ensure that all the available resources are put to best use, consumer choice and involvement are enhanced, and flexible services are provided which are tailored to individual need.

3.1.5 The following sections of this chapter consider each of these responsibilities in further detail. To discharge them, each local authority will need to ensure that it has in place an integrated system for assessment and decision-making within a clear budgetary framework.

3.2 ASSESSMENT

3.2.1 It is not the Government's intention that anyone and everyone needing some form of care in the community should be referred to social services departments. People with exclusively health care needs which can be met in the community will continue to have direct access to, and receive service directly from, the community and primary health services. Some people's needs for social care will be relatively slight and they can be helped with straightforward advice and information. Some will have rights under current disablement legislation. Local authorities will need to form their own views about when a formalised assessment process becomes necessary.

3.2.2 The rest of this section is about people whose needs extend beyond health care to include social care and support eg for mobility, personal care, domestic tasks, financial affairs, accommodation, leisure and employment, which they cannot arrange for themselves. For those people, social services authorities will be responsible for arranging an assessment of the individual's needs for community care, taking account of their problems, needs and circumstances. Assessments should apply both to people seeking domiciliary and day care services, and to people seeking admission to residential or nursing home care.

Principles of Assessment

3.2.3 The objective of assessment is to determine the best available way to help the individual. Assessments should focus positively on what the individual can and cannot do, and could be expected to achieve, taking account of his or her personal and social relationships. Assessment should not focus only on the user's suitability for a particular existing service. The aim should be first to review the possibility of enabling the individual to continue to live at home even if this means arranging a move to different accommodation within the local community, and if that possibility does not exist, to consider whether residential or nursing home care would be appropriate.

3.2.4 Some individuals will suffer not from a single problem or disability, but from several, covering both social and health care needs. In those cases no single professional discipline can encompass the whole picture. The assessment procedure will therefore need to be flexible enough to be able to take as broad a view of the situation as necessary.

3.2.5 All agencies and professions involved with the individual and his or her problems should be brought into the assessment procedure when necessary. These may include social workers, GPs, community nurses, hospital staff such as consultants in geriatric medicine, psychiatry, rehabilitation and other hospital specialties, nurses, physiotherapists, occupational therapists, speech therapists, continence advisers, community psychiatric nurses, staff involved with vision and hearing impairment, housing officers, the Employment Department's Resettlement Officers and its Employment Rehabilitation Service, home helps, home care assistants and voluntary workers.

3.2.6 Assessments should take account of the wishes of the individual and his or her carer, and of the carer's ability to continue to provide care, and where possible should include their active participation. Effort should be made to offer flexible services which enable individuals and carers to make choices.

The Organisation of Assessments

3.2.7 The Government proposes that the responsibility for ensuring that an assessment is made should be a specific duty of the local authority. This does not mean that other agencies should be excluded, nor that local authorities can or should make decisions on services managed by other agencies. A single individual should be responsible for ensuring that each case is dealt with effectively. Indeed, an essential skill which case co-ordinators will need to deploy will be to manage the involvement, contribution, co-operation and partnership between the local authority and the other authorities and professions involved in providing services. The Government expects all those concerned to contribute positively to such arrangements.

3.2.8 There are a number of ways in which an individual may seek help and may therefore need an individual assessment. For example, he or she may apply for local authority home care services or a place in a local authority residential care home, or may request services under the Disabled Persons (Services, Consultation and Representation) Act 1986. In addition, it will now be possible for an individual to ask for local authority funding towards the cost of a place in a private residential or nursing home, or for the provision of domiciliary care. Local authorities should aim to develop a common process for all these situations,and to ensure that an individual is offered the help needed irrespective of the basis on which their first contact with the authority is made.

3.2.9 There will be a wide range of referral routes, or entry points, into the assessment procedure and local authorities should ensure that means of referral are widely publicised. They should also establish, and make public, criteria of eligibility for assessment, and the way in which their assessment processes will work.

3.2.10 Local authorities will have the duty of establishing their own cost-effective assessment procedures. The Government believes that effective schemes can best be achieved by allowing authorities the flexibility to take account of local factors and strengths.

3.2.11 Each assessment should, of course, be handled on its merits, but simplicity should be the key. Contributions can be sought quickly and informally and it is not always necessary for all contributors to attend meetings. Assessments should be carried out timeously. The Government does not wish to see an elaborate and bureaucratic pattern of costly and time-consuming case conferences established, nor does it want to see a duplication of effort. For instance, where a patient has already been assessed for discharge from hospital, this should form the basis of the assessment decision.

Action Following an Assessment

3.2.12 The aim of assessment should be to arrive at a decision on whether services should be provided, and in what form. Assessments will therefore have to be made against a background of stated objectives and priorities determined by the local authority. Decisions on service provision will have to take account of what is available and affordable. Priority must be given to those whose needs are greatest. As part of its planning machinery, every local authority should monitor the outcomes of its assessment process, and the implications of these outcomes for future development of services.

Information and Training

3.2.13 The new assessment arrangements will involve significant changes in the way professional workers are expected to operate. The Government proposes four measures to facilitate this:

- it will publish a detailed code of guidance for local authorities, copied to health authorities, to advise on the workings of the new assessment system. This will be issued in late 1990, following discussions with professionals and representative bodies;

- each local authority will be expected to publish a local guide to the principles and workings of the assessment procedure. This should be made available to all those involved in assessments, to local agencies (including voluntary groups) and to members of the public;

- the training needs of all those involved will be discussed by the Department of Health, the Local Authority Associations, and relevant professional and representative bodies.

- the Social Services Inspectorate will monitor progress, collaborating where appropriate with other relevant bodies.

3.3 DESIGNING SERVICES TO MEET INDIVIDUAL NEED

Responsibilities of Social Services Authorities

3.3.1 Once an individual assessment has been completed, and a decision has been taken that publicly funded care can and should be arranged, it will be the responsibility of the social services authority to design care arrangements in line with individual needs, in consultation with the client and other care professionals, and within available resources. Decisions will need to take account of the local availability and pattern of services as well as any sources of support available in the community - whether from family, friends, neighbours or local voluntary organisations - and should seek where necessary to provide assistance and respite for the carer.

Case Management

3.3.2 People's care needs may change over time and therefore need to be monitored. Where an individual's needs are complex or significant levels of resources are involved, the Government sees considerable merit in nominating a "case manager" to take responsibility for ensuring that individuals' needs are regularly reviewed, resources are managed effectively and that each service user has a single point of contact. The "case manager" will often be employed by the social services authority, but this need not always be so. He or she may or may not be the designated person responsible for the original assessment and design stages.

3.3.3 Case management provides an effective method of targeting resources and planning services to meet specific needs of individual clients. The approach has been successfully employed in a number of schemes and projects, some of the best known of which are in Kent, Gateshead and Durham. Case management systems have also been an important feature of a number of the Department of Health's Care in the Community Pilot Projects launched in 1983. The Government believes that the wider introduction of the key principles of case management would confer considerable benefit, and will seek to encourage their application more widely.

3.3.4 To be effective case management should include:

- identification of people in need, including systems for referral
- assessment of care needs
- planning and securing the delivery of care
- monitoring the quality of care provided
- review of client needs.

It is not essential that the same manager should undertake all these tasks for a particular client but a clearly identified individual should be designated for each function. The Government does not wish to be prescriptive about the background from which the case manager should be drawn. A range of backgrounds could be possible, although social workers, home care organisers or community nurses, as the professionals in most regular contact with the client, may be particularly suitable.

3.3.5 The Government also sees advantage in linking case management with delegated responsibility for budgetary management. This need not be pursued down to the level of each individual client in all cases, but - used flexibly - is an important way of enabling those closest to the identification of client needs to make the best possible use of the resources available.

3.3.6 Social services authorities will be expected to indicate in their community care plans how they propose to apply case management techniques, and develop clear budgetary systems.

3.4 SECURING THE DELIVERY OF SERVICES

3.4.1 Once a package of care has been designed, it will be the responsibility of the social services authority to ensure that the agreed services are in place. Health authorities and other agencies will be expected to arrange the delivery of any components of care which they have agreed to provide as part of the package. The Government will expect local authorities to make use wherever possible of services from voluntary, "not for profit" and private providers insofar as this represents a cost effective care choice. Social services authorities will continue to play a valuable role in the provision of services, but in those cases where they are still the main or sole providers of services, they will be expected to take all reasonable steps to secure diversity of provision.

3.4.2 In particular, it will be essential for local authorities to develop the capacity to purchase places in independently run homes. No local authority should deprive those people assessed as needing residential care of the opportunity to enter an independently run home meeting the required standards of care.

The Enabling Authority

3.4.3 Stimulating the development of non-statutory service providers will result in a range of benefits for the consumer, in particular:

- a wider range of choice of services;
- services which meet individual needs in a more flexible and innovative way;
- competition between providers, resulting in better value for money and a more cost-effective service.

The Government envisages, however, that the statutory sector will continue to play an important role in backing up, developing and monitoring private and voluntary care facilities, and providing services where this remains the best way of meeting care needs.

3.4.4 At present, private sector activity is largely concentrated in the residential care and nursing home field. Non-statutory provision of domiciliary and day care services and respite care is less well-developed and, with the exception of some voluntary sector activity, people have far less choice in this sector. The

Government would welcome greater diversification by private providers and believes that its proposals for funding and assessment should help to stimulate this. Many local authorities are already moving to grasp these opportunities, but the Government expects social services authorities to explore ways of further stimulating private and voluntary provision of domiciliary, day and respite care wherever possible.

3.4.5 Social services authorities will be expected to make clear in their community care plans what steps they will be taking to make increased use of non-statutory service providers or, where such providers are not currently available, how they propose to stimulate such activity. In particular, they should consider how they will encourage diversification into the non-residential care sector. Local authorities should ensure that the experience gained by voluntary organisations in the development of respite care (whether planned or to deal with a crisis) is fully available through the partnerships they devise.

Developing a Mixed Economy of Care

3.4.6 There are a number of ways authorities can promote the mixed economy of care including:

- determining clear specifications of service requirements, and arrangements for tenders and contracts;
- taking steps to stimulate the setting up of "not for profit" agencies;
- identifying areas of their own work which are sufficiently self-contained to be suitable for "floating off" as self-managing units;
- stimulating the development of new voluntary sector activity.

3.4.7 The Government believes that the wider use of service specification and tendering is likely to be one of the most effective ways of stimulating the non-statutory sector. It has decided against extending compulsory competitive tendering to social care services, and favours giving local authorities an opportunity to make greater use of service specifications, agency agreements and contracts in an evolutionary way. The Government believes that this will have the beneficial effect of requiring authorities to define desired outcomes; to be more specific about the nature of the service they are seeking to provide to achieve those outcomes; and to define the necessary inputs.

3.4.8 This in turn will require an improvement in information gathering systems and a more vigorous approach to management which is likely to require a clear distinction to be made between the purchasing and providing functions within a local authority. Local authorities will need to give priority to developing purchasing systems for private residential and nursing home care.

Quality

3.4.9 It will be essential that, whenever they purchase services, social services authorities should take steps to ensure that the quality to be delivered is clearly specified and properly monitored, bearing in mind that vulnerable people are involved as users. The authority should be clear in advance how it will deal with a situation where a contractor is not providing an acceptable service.

3.4.10 Where these do not already exist, authorities should establish procedures for receiving comments and complaints from users of services. Procedures should be publicised. They will be an essential safeguard for users and will also act as an important monitoring and management instrument for social services authorities and service providers alike.

3.4.11 The Government will expect local authorities to retain the ability to act as direct service providers, if other forms of service provision are unforthcoming or unsuitable. In order to do this, the local authority will need to retain capacity, skill and experience in key service provision functions. This is likely to be particularly important in services for people with high levels of dependency, or particularly challenging patterns of behaviour, whose care it is essential to safeguard.

The Voluntary Sector

3.4.12 Sir Roy Griffiths identified the need for a clearer basis for funding the voluntary sector if its potential contribution to community care was to be developed further. He recommended that there should be clear agreement between the public agency and the voluntary or "not-for-profit" body, either on a fee per client basis, or through a contract laying down a given level of service. The Government agrees with Sir Roy's approach and will expect public funding agencies to develop an increasingly contractual relationship with the voluntary bodies they fund. This will serve to:

- clarify the role of voluntary agencies;
- give them a sounder financial base and allow them a greater degree of certainty in planning for the future;
- enhance the development of more flexible and cost-effective forms of non-statutory provision.

3.4.13 Authorities should seek to move towards contractual funding in partnership with the voluntary sector. Voluntary organisations may need to make major changes in their working methods and there is likely to be considerable advantage for both sides of the partnership if the voluntary sector can be involved at an early stage in negotiation over the contents of the contract. The policy base on which contracts are to be drawn up should be clearly specified and understood by all concerned.

3.4.14 The Government also recognises that some important voluntary sector activities may not be suitable for a contractual funding approach, including, for example, developmental work, advocacy, campaigning and education. It will be important to allow scope for the emergence of new, small-scale groups and to avoid the over predominance of large, well established voluntary bodies. For both these purposes, health and local authorities may continue to make grants towards the administrative expenses of voluntary organisations.

3.5 Housing and Community Care

3.5.1 If dependent people are to be helped to continue living in the community, then their homes must be places where it is possible to provide the care they need. The Government believes that housing is a vital component of community care and it is often the key to independent living. Over half of the people aged over 65 are now owner-occupiers. It is important that they receive advice and help at the right time to enable them to go on living in their own homes for as long as possible. That is why the Government supports the provision by local authorities, housing associations and voluntary bodies of local care and repair, and staying put, schemes. These advise elderly people on how to keep their homes in good repair and on finance for repairs and adaptations, for example by using the capital tied up in their property. The Local Government and Housing Bill also contains measures which enable local housing authorities to provide specific assistance - grants and materials - to help elderly people, or those caring for them, with minor works in their homes.

3.5.2 With increasing disability, people may only be able to stay in their own homes if these are suitably adapted. Adaptations may include the provision of hand rails, chairlifts and alarm systems connected to sheltered housing and the availability of wardens. They may also include more substantial adaptations to the structure of the dwelling. In 1987/88 local housing authorities in England gave grants totalling £45 million to help disabled people carry out structural adaptations to 25,000 homes. The Local Government and Housing Bill builds on this by including provision for an entirely new income-related disabled facilities grant. This will be mandatory primarily where improvements are needed to give access to basic amenities in and around the home. It will also be possible to give grants for making dwellings suitable for the accommodation, welfare or employment of a disabled person. These grants are in addition to those available to people on low incomes for essential repairs and improvements.

3.5.3 People who are more severely disabled might be helped by a move into some form of specialised accommodation, such as purpose designed housing for people in wheelchairs, or core and cluster developments for people with mental handicaps. There are also various forms of sheltered and very sheltered housing for elderly disabled people. This option should be primarily for those who want and need it, after an assessment of their care needs.

3.5.4 Social Services authorities will need to work closely with housing authorities, housing associations and other providers of housing of all types in developing plans for a full and flexible range of housing. Where necessary, housing needs should form part of the assessment of care needs and the occupational therapist may have a key role here.

3.6 DOMICILIARY AND DAY CARE SERVICES

3.6.1 A range of domiciliary and day care services and facilities, at present largely the responsibility of social services authorities, are available to enable people to continue to live in the community. These include help with personal care and domestic tasks such as dressing, cleaning, washing and preparing meals; with transport, budgeting, disability equipment and adaptations to homes; and with basic daily living. In addition, day care, respite care and leisure facilities are available to provide support for individuals and carers.

3.6.2 However, the provision of such services is uneven and poorly co-ordinated and there is a tendency to match clients to services, rather than services to client needs. Recent work undertaken by the Social Services Inspectorate has revealed considerable variations in the level of resources allocated to home care services, and poor targeting of available resources. There is great scope for establishing clear policy frameworks and guidance for resource use, and for increasing the provision of more flexible and intensive personal care services for people who would otherwise require institutional care.

3.6.3 The Government believes that the range and diversity of domiciliary care services can be greatly increased by enabling those responsible for planning, managing and delivering the services to operate flexibly. Delegation of responsibilities for resource management to local level, and the encouragement of tendering for certain services, are means of stimulating the growth of new domiciliary and day care services in the independent sector. This should enable case managers to draw on a more varied network of service provision when constructing packages of care for individuals.

3.7 RESIDENTIAL AND NURSING HOME CARE

Role of Residential and Nursing Home Care

3.7.1 Residential care homes and nursing homes will continue to play an important part in meeting people's care needs. Some people will always need more support than can be reasonably provided in their own homes or in sheltered housing. For them, depending on the nature of the care they require, residential or nursing home care may be the best choice. The Government believes that entering residential or nursing home care should always be a positive choice made in the light of an assessment of an individual's needs and circumstances.

Securing Places

3.7.2 From April 1991 local authorities will be responsible, in collaboration with health care professionals, for assessing the needs of new applicants for public support for residential or nursing home care. If, after assessment, it is decided that a residential care or nursing home place represents the right choice for the person involved, it will be the responsibility of the social services authority to arrange a place in a suitable home. The type of home to be chosen should be dependent on the outcome of the assessment; a nursing home place should be secured only if the assessment establishes a need for nursing care as the whole or main component of the care required.

3.7.3 Social services authorities will be expected to make maximum possible use of independent providers of residential and nursing home care when arranging placements. The authority will need to estimate the number of places it will need, and then make arrangements for meeting projected demand. There will be no nationally set limits to the level of fees which may be met by local authorities; it will be for each authority to exercise its own purchasing power to achieve best value for money.

3.7.4 There may be a number of ways of achieving this. The authority could, for example, negotiate fees with an individual home for an agreed number of places or it could set limits for the level of fees it is willing to pay. Contracts will need to be drawn up very carefully and will need to specify precisely the level and quality of service required. Specifications might usefully require service providers to set up and operate systems for evaluating their own performance. Procedures for monitoring and evaluating performance should also be clearly stated at the outset.

3.7.5 The Government believes that the introduction of competitive tendering disciplines to the residential care and nursing home field will enhance the ability of social services authorities to obtain best value for public money. They will be in a strong position to use their new found purchasing power to ensure high quality care for those people who really need it.

Paying for Places

3.7.6 Under the new funding arrangements, the local authority may enter into a contractual agreement with an independent provider. Once a price has been negotiated and agreed, the social services authority will itself directly meet the charges levied by the home. The authority will then be required to assess the ability of each individual to contribute towards the cost of the care they will be receiving. In the majority of cases an assessment of the applicant's income will already have been carried out for social security purposes. People receiving Income Support and/or Housing Benefit, will be required to pay these benefits and any other income over to the social services authority, save for that sum which is to be set aside as a personal allowance (see 3.8.5)

3.7.7 The Government recognises that this payment system, involving assessment of each applicant's financial means, will result in some extra work for social services authorities. However, the system builds on existing arrangements for current local authority sponsored residents of homes and for the residents in local authority managed homes. The Government believes that it will prove the most satisfactory way for arranging payments for all types of residents and for home owners. The Government intends to consult the Local Authority Associations on the detailed working of these arrangements.

Consumer Choice

3.7.8 For many people, entering residential care or a nursing home will mean moving permanently from their own homes and neighbourhoods where they may have lived for a long time. This can be a difficult step but one which may be made easier if approached positively. The Government believes that, subject to the availability of resources, people should be able to exercise the maximum possible choice about the home they enter. The preferences of relatives and other carers should also be taken carefully into account. If relatives or friends wish, and are able, to make a contribution towards the cost of care, an individual may decide to look for a place in a more expensive home. The arrangements made by the social services authority should be sufficiently flexible to permit this.

3.7.9 The Government recognises that some people will wish to enter a home in an area other than that in which they normally live, for example to move nearer to family or friends. Subject to the availability of resources, people will continue to be able to choose to do this under the new funding arrangements. As with other applicants, their needs will be assessed by the social services authority in the area in which they are ordinarily resident and, if judged to be in need of residential or nursing home care, the assessing authority will indicate how much it is able to pay towards the costs of care, either allowing the individual to make their own arrangements if they so choose, or making arrangements directly with the local authority in the area into which the applicant wishes to move.

Local Authority Homes

3.7.10 The arrangements for paying social security benefits to people in local authority homes will not change as a result of the new proposals. The Government wishes to ensure that local authorities have every incentive to make use of the independent sector when placing people in residential settings. Local authorities will therefore continue to meet the full cost of maintaining people in authorities' own homes, including the costs of accommodation and food.

3.7.11 All authorities will need to review the extent to which they need to maintain homes of their own in these circumstances. Some rationalisation is likely to be required.

Care for People with Terminal Illness

3.7.12 Arrangements for planning and co-ordinating the provision of hospice - type care for patients suffering from a terminal illness will continue to be the responsibility of health authorities, whether they use their own facilities, or those provided by voluntary or private organisations.

3.8 CHARGES FOR SERVICES

3.8.1 Under present arrangements local authorities are required to charge what residents in homes can afford, up to the full economic cost of their care. Authorities are able, but not required, to charge for day and domiciliary care. These arrangements will be preserved. In practice many consumers of personal social services cannot afford the full cost of the service, and ability to pay does not and should not in any way influence decisions on the services to be provided. This accords with the Government's general policy on charges for local services: those able to meet all or part of the economic cost should be expected to do so. Moreover, effective costing and charging procedures can be valuable in achieving the best use of resources across the range of personal social services and local social services authorities will be expected to develop them.

Residential and Nursing Home Care

3.8.2 Local authorities are required under the National Assistance Act 1948 Section 22 to charge the full economic cost of residential care where residents can afford to pay, and the method of determining ability to pay is prescribed nationally. These arrangements will continue and will be applied to meeting the costs in independent residential and nursing homes when local authorities take over this responsibility in April 1991.

3.8.3 At present the rules for assessing the ability to pay of residents in local authority homes are different from - and on the whole less generous than - the rules which apply to residents in independent homes under income support arrangements. The opportunity will be taken to remove this anomaly: from April 1991 the rules governing assessment of ability to pay under income support arrangements will apply also to residents in local authority homes.

3.8.4 All residents in care homes and nursing homes supported from public funds are entitled to a personal allowance. The amount fixed under income support arrangements is slightly higher than local authorities can allow. The Government proposes that the same entitlement to a personal allowance will apply to all residents supported from public funds in all homes, local authority, voluntary and private. The rate of the allowance will be linked to that payable at present to income support claimants in independent homes.

Other Personal Social Services

3.8.5 Local authorities have statutory powers to charge for other personal social services for adults (Health and Social Services and Social Security Adjudications Act 1983 Section 17). If a user represents that they cannot afford to pay the charge the local authority are statutorily required to reduce the charge to such amount (if any) as appears reasonable to them. The Government proposes to preserve these arrangements, which will apply equally to services provided through other agencies. This provision permits charging for home help, home care, meals provision and day care services. Local authorities also provide other services for which it would not be appropriate to charge including social work support, occupational therapy, advice and assessment of client needs. These services, including assessments under the new arrangements described in 3.2.1 - 3.2.13, will continue to be provided free of charge.

CHAPTER FOUR: ROLES AND RESPONSIBILITIES OF THE HEALTH SERVICE

CHAPTER FOUR: ROLES AND RESPONSIBILITIES OF THE HEALTH SERVICE

The Health Component of Community Care

4.1 Community care is about the health as well as the social needs of the population. Health care, in its broadest sense, is an essential component of the range of services which may be needed to help people to continue to live in their own homes for as long as possible.

4.2 The key functions and responsibilities of the health service as a whole remain essentially unaltered by the proposals in this White Paper. "Working for Patients" explained that it would be the responsibility of health authorities to ensure that the health needs of the population for which they are responsible are met. To achieve this they will need to work closely with Family Practitioner Committees (to be known in future as Family Practitioner Service Authorities). Health authorities will remain responsible for the health care needs of those people who also have a need for social care. Such people may well have special needs for health care, whether for primary care or acute hospital care, or for long-term care. Their handicap or disability may also make them heavy consumers of health care. In some individual cases it may well be difficult to draw a clear distinction between the needs of an individual for health and for social care. In such cases it will be critically important for the responsible authorities to work together.

4.3 The Government endorses Sir Roy Griffiths' recommendations for the responsibilities of Regional and District Health Authorities. Their responsibility for ensuring the provision of health care covers investigation, diagnosis, treatment, rehabilitation and continuing care, together with - most importantly - community health services, including community nursing. The primary responsibility here will be with District Health Authorities, who will each be responsible for their own residents. They may meet those responsibilities by placing contracts for services provided by their own directly managed Units or by other DHAs, National Health Service Trusts, the private sector, or other agencies. Health authorities also have a responsibility for health promotion and the prevention of ill-health which should in time influence future needs for community care.

4.4 The Government recognises that the primary health care services, including, dental, pharmaceutical, ophthalmic, chiropody, and therapy services, make an important contribution to community care, both through their health promotion work and in providing care and treatment for people living in the community. The GP has a particularly important contribution to make which is considered in 4.11-4.13 below.

4.5 Some people will continue to have medical or nursing needs which cannot be met in the community. Depending on the nature of their condition, they may need acute hospital care for a time or they may require longer-term hospital or nursing home care. The responsibilities of the NHS for the provision of continuous care are set out in 4.19-4.22.

4.6 Acute hospital care, long-stay care and community care should be complementary and should be planned to provide a co-ordinated range of services. It continues to be the responsibility of the Health Authority to ensure that discharge procedures are in place and agreed with the local authority so that people can return home with the support they need or move to appropriate care.

Community Care Responsibilities

4.7 In addition to their responsibilities for the provision of health care, health authorities and family practitioner committees will be expected to make specific contributions to the new arrangements for community care. These include:

Assessment

4.8 In future, it will be the responsibility of social services authorities to ensure that multi-disciplinary assessments are made where necessary to enable them to discharge their responsibilities. Assessment will need to be made available for people currently (and perhaps inappropriately) receiving long-term hospital care who may need social care in future. Health authorities will be expected to make the necessary contribution to these procedures by ensuring that health experts such as clinicians, community nurses and therapists are made available to take part in assessment. Contracts between health authorities and health care providers will need to take account of this. GPs will be expected to make a similar contribution.

Collaboration with Local Authorities

4.9 The Government's proposals for community care positively reinforce the need for health authorities and family practitioner committees to collaborate with local authorities in planning and providing community services. Effective joint working and planning will continue to be essential. Chapter 6 sets out the Government's approach to collaboration.

Production of Community Care Plans

4.10 Health authorities will be expected to prepare plans setting out their community care policies and the provision they intend to make for community services and community care. The form, content and proposals for monitoring these plans are considered further in Chapter 5.

The role of the GP

4.11 The Government recognises the key role played by general practitioners in caring for people in the community. GPs will often be the first to know when someone's situation or condition changes. Family doctors can bring together physical, psychological and social factors when considering health and illness. They practice in co-operation with both medical and non-medical colleagues, and know how and when to intervene through treatment, prevention and education to promote the health of patients and their families.

4.12 The Government believes that GPs are well placed to ensure that factors other than medical ones which affect the quality of life are taken into consideration. Practising near to their patients' homes, family doctors see the majority of their elderly and ill patients several times a year. At least in the better practices, most problems of ill health and social handicap are well-known and where primary health care teams work effectively the community nurses and health visitors also play a full part. The Government's new contract for general practitioners builds on this foundation. GPs will be expected, under their terms of service, to offer a visit to those aged 75 or over to see their home environment, find out whether carers and relatives are available and to assess social, physical and mental well-being. Under paragraph 13 of the terms of service general practitioners are under an obligation to refer on patients where there are problems needing specialist services, for example the assistance of a geriatrician, and also to provide advice to enable patients to take advantage of local authority social services.

4.13 Close working relationships between GPs and social services authorities are already well established in many areas and GPs are called upon to make a contribution to assessment procedures for community care. Where these are not already in place the Government wishes to see the development of clearly agreed local arrangements to enable individual GPs to make their full contribution to community care. Complex and bureaucratic procedures should be avoided.

Community Health Services and the Role of Community Nurses

4.14 The Government recognises that achieving the aim of ensuring that more people are looked after in their own homes for a longer period is likely to involve greater demands on the community health services. Community nursing care, therapy services, and services such as chiropody all have a part to play in enabling people to remain in the community.

4.15 Community nursing services include health visitors, district nurses, community psychiatric and mental handicap nurses who bring to their work a variety of skills and expert knowledge. They are able to assist people with social, psychological and health care problems which may affect their quality of life. As community workers, nurses are in close touch with the network of help available in a neighbourhood and can mobilise resources to respond sensitively to people's needs.

4.16 Community nursing staff play a vital role at present in the delivery of community care. The Government's proposals seek to build on their existing contribution. The trust and confidence which often exists between patient and nurse can be particularly valuable. Nurses represent an important resource and it will be essential in future that health authorities, social services and voluntary bodies make best use of their time and skills.

4.17 The White Paper sets out a number of areas where community nurses can make an important contribution, including:

- assessment procedures in which nurses may need to take an active part;
- the development of care arrangements. Social Services authorities will need to take nursing advice where necessary. In some cases nurses may be well placed to act as key workers for those clients with whom they are in the most regular contact and they should be willing to do so, where appropriate;
- the provision of care once a package of services has been designed. District Health Authorities will need to ensure that community nurses are able to discharge these responsibilities.

4.18 The Government wishes to ensure that nurses' time is deployed to best effect on work which requires their special skills, leaving work which does not require those skills to be done by others. Training authorities may wish to adapt existing training programmes and consider providing such training in a multi-disciplinary setting in order to enhance understanding between health and social services professionals.

The Role of the NHS in Providing Continuous Health Care

4.19 The aim of health authorities should be to ensure that community health services are available to enable people to live in their own homes for as long as possible. Health Authorities are therefore expected to continue to develop their community health services in line with this objective.

4.20 There will, however, always be some people who cannot be supported in their own homes. Where such people require continuous care for reasons of ill-health, it will remain the responsibility of health authorities to provide for this. Examples here might include mentally ill people who require specialised residential health provision; as, indeed, may some people with mental or physical handicaps. Some frail elderly people may require continuous health care, traditionally provided in long-stay hospital wards, which exist in parallel with the provision of nursing care by the private health sector.

4.21 Health authorities will need to ensure that their plans allow for the provision of continuous residential health care for those highly dependent people who need it. The Government believes that such services should be provided for those who need them, but that people should not be placed in this type of care unnecessarily. Whether this requires an increase or a reduction in the level of continuous health care provided through the NHS will depend very much on local circumstances. Each health authority should agree the level of continuous care it proposes to provide or arrange for its own population with the relevant local authorities to ensure that health and local authority plans are compatible and comprehensive. Health authorities should then publish their proposals in their community care plans.

4.22 For many people who enter long-term care within the NHS, this will effectively become their home for the remaining years of their lives. The Government believes that continuous care is best provided in small units, which can develop a more home-like atmosphere than is often possible in wards in large hospitals. Such units can offer patients their own room or personal space, and an informal style of care, without, for example, a formal daily timetable or staff uniforms.

Care for People with Terminal Illness

4.23 As now, health authorities will be responsible for the medical and nursing component of care for people who are terminally ill. Support for hospice care will also remain with health authorities. Social services authorities will continue to have responsibility for arranging the social care and support which may be needed by terminally ill people living in the community.

Managing the Transition

4.24 Much progress has already been made in providing health and social care in a community setting for people who previously were being cared for in a hospital or institutional setting. But there are still people at present in hospitals and similar institutions whose prime need is for social care, or who would benefit from a move to a smaller residential care unit. The responsibility for ensuring the care of such people could thus move from the health authority to the local authority. It will therefore be necessary for health authorities and local authorities to continue work together to develop comprehensive and compatible arrangements for the care of discharged patients - as well as for new "customers" in the future.

Resources Transferred to Develop Community Services

4.25 The system whereby health authorities may offer lump-sum payments or continuing grants to local authorities or voluntary organisations in respect of people moving from hospital to community care is to remain undisturbed. Health authorities may wish to continue to enter into agreements with local authorities which enable funds to be transferred as responsibility for arranging care moves from health to local authority. Regional Health Authorities will have a strategic role to play in ensuring that consistent arrangements are in place. Such funding agreements might usefully be set out in the community care plans produced by each authority.

CHAPTER FIVE: ACHIEVING HIGH STANDARDS OF CARE

CHAPTER FIVE: ACHIEVING HIGH STANDARDS OF CARE

The Role of the Centre

5.1 Securing and safeguarding the necessary quality of services must be a central objective for all agencies involved in the delivery of community care. People in need of community care are vulnerable and their interests should be protected. The Department of Health, in partnership with local authorities, health authorities and other interested agencies, will play an important part in helping to maintain, and where necessary improve, the quality of care provided.

5.2 Clarifying responsibilities, establishing where accountability for service delivery lies and specifying service requirements for contracts, will all help to keep attention focused on the quality and suitability of services. The Government proposes to take a number of steps to be able to satisfy itself that authorities have plans in line with national objectives, and to monitor performance against those plans.

5.3 The Government will bring proposals before Parliament to:

- require local authorities to draw up and publish plans for community care services, in consultation with health authorities and other interested agencies;
- enable the Secretary of State for Health to call for reports and information from local authorities where he has reason to think these may be needed, and to specify the form in which they are to be provided;
- enable the Secretary of State for Health to issue directions and give guidance over the full range of personal social services activities by local authorities.

5.4 These powers will provide the basis of new planning and monitoring arrangements for community care. The Government has no intention of establishing an over-bureaucratic or heavily centralised system. Its aim will be to satisfy itself that authorities are developing and implementing plans in line with national objectives and priorities, at a reasonable pace. For that purpose the Social Services Inspectorate will play an active part in inspecting plans, monitoring performance and offering advice and guidance to authorities and the Secretary of State. Where necessary, the Government will not hesitate to intervene in order to stimulate improvements.

5.5 The remainder of this chapter sets out in further detail the Government's proposals for the new planning and monitoring system, for safeguarding the quality of social care provision and for the inspection of residential care and nursing homes.

Local Authority Community Care Plans

5.6 Local authorities will need to have clear plans for the development of their community care provision against which their performance can be monitored and assessed. The purpose of such plans will be to enable social services authorities to:

- set out strategic objectives and priorities and, over realistic planning periods, set specific targets, in collaboration with relevant agencies;
- take account of the needs of people who have been in hospital a long time, and need help to re-establish themselves away from large institutional settings;
- assess other local needs, taking account of the results of assessments in individual cases;
- organise their move away from the role of exclusive service provider to that of service arranger and procurer;
- ensure that service arrangements respect and preserve individual independence, include adequate quality control systems, offer freedom of choice, and provide services in a sensitive and responsive way;
- monitor performance; and inform the public.

5.7 Social services authorities, as well as health authorities, family practitioner committees and housing authorities, will be expected to ensure that their community care plans complement each other and do not conflict. Authorities should also consult with, and take account of the views of, private and voluntary sector service providers and representatives of service users and carers in drawing up their plans.

5.8 Community care plans should be public documents intended to communicate an authority's policies and plans to the widest possible audience in as straightforward a manner as possible. Plans should therefore be produced in a format which is useful and informative to those outside the local authority.

The Planning Timetable

5.9 The Government's intention is that community care plans should be produced by 1 April 1991 and reviewed annually to a timetable compatible with local financial planning cycles. The financial planning cycle already provides authorities with a framework for the consideration of planning intentions, and aligning the two processes will enable account to be taken of the resource implications. Plans covering a three year period should be the norm. The annual review process will ensure that in each financial year there will be an up-to-date three year plan.

Contents of Plan

5.10 The first plans will inevitably concentrate on the management and delivery of the key changes set out in this White Paper. In particular, social services authorities will be expected to set out:-

- their assessment of the needs of the population they serve;
- their strategic objectives for community care in the next three years and how these relate to national policy objectives;

- how they intend to identify and meet their needs for the information on which to base planning;
- the arrangements for assessments of individual applicants for care, and how they are integrated with the budgetary framework;
- how the new purchasing tasks are to be organised and managed, including budgetary arrangements;
- how services for people at home, including their carers, are to be improved;
- how they have co-ordinated plans and activities with those of health authorities, family practitioner committees and housing authorities;
- what arrangements they will make for case management;
- what information is to be provided to service users and their carers about services;
- what training is to be provided for relevant staff groups;
- how the contribution of the independent sector is to be stimulated;
- how and when inspection and registration units will be established;
- what quality assurance and systems for safeguarding service standards are to be established, including complaints procedures.

5.11 The Department of Health will need to assure itself that community care plans are in line with national policies, and that the above elements are in place.

Health Authority Plans

5.12 Health authorities will be expected to prepare plans setting out their community care policies and the arrangements they propose for securing community services and community care. It will be for health authorities to decide whether these plans would best form part of their overall plans or should be produced separately as a joint exercise with the relevant local authorities. But their key contents and resource assumptions will need to be shared and agreed with the social services authority. The plans should be public documents.

5.13 Health authorities will be accountable for ensuring the provision of the services to which these plans commit them, and their performance will be monitored - in the case of District Health Authorities, by Regional Health Authorities and by the Department of Health through the Regional Review System.

Monitoring the Quality of Social Care

5.14 Monitoring the quality of services will become more complex as social services authorities' responsibilities for arranging the provision of community care increase. As purchasers, arrangers and providers of care services local authorities must be responsible for ensuring adequate systems are in place for securing the necessary quality of services, and monitoring it over time.

5.15 The purchasing discipline will itself help to achieve this end, because it will require services to be specified in detail as part of a contract, which should also include provision for monitoring and break-clauses in the event of service specification not being met. Other arrangements, including a clearly defined and well-publicised complaints system, will need to be made. The Department of Health will need to satisfy itself that adequate quality control systems are included in local authorities' community care plans.

5.16 Social services authorities will be assisted by the Government's 3 year development programme, now under way, aimed at testing and promoting ways of improving quality of life for people in residential care. The programme is based on recommendations in the report of the committee chaired by Lady Wagner "Residential Care: A Positive Choice". This programme aims at better training for staff in homes, better information for users in making choices, effective, readily accessible arrangements for making suggestions and complaints, a closer relationship between homes and their local communities and better management of homes.

Inspection of Residential Care and Nursing Homes

5.17 Arrangements already exist under the Registered Homes Act 1984 to safeguard people in independent residential care and nursing homes. The Government does not propose to alter these arrangements for nursing homes. Independent residential homes are subject to registration and inspection by local authority social service departments. This has given rise to concern about the standards required by local authorities in carrying out these duties, by comparison with the standards required or achieved in local authority homes.

5.18 The Government believes that common standards should apply across all sectors. To assist this, it proposes that local authorities should set up independent inspection units, under the Director of Social Services, charged with inspecting and reporting on both local authority and registerable independent residential care homes.

5.19 These units would be independent of the day to day management of local authority homes and would be accountable direct to the Director of Social Services. They would be expected to apply the same quality assurance criteria to all homes. The organisation and method of operation of these units will depend to some extent on the size of authority and the number of homes to be inspected.

5.20 The units should include inspectors recruited from outside the social services department: for example former owners or managers in the independent sector or former public sector staff experienced in residential care.

5.21 Local authorities may wish to call upon these units to inspect service provision (residential and otherwise) by agencies under contract.

5.22 There will be consultations with local authority and independent sector interests on the detail of what is proposed. These will cover such matters as the organisation and management of the inspection units, arrangements for submission and scrutiny of reports, follow-up of reports, recruitment of some inspection staff from outside the local authority and reports to the social services committee on the activities of the unit.

5.23 There will need to be provision for representatives of the private and voluntary sectors, and residents of homes, to have a voice in the organisation, management and operation of registration and inspection activities. Proposals for achieving this will be included in the consultation document.

5.24 The Department of Health proposes to issue further guidance for registration and inspection staff on the conditions to be expected in a good home, after consultation with local authority and independent sector interests. The guidance will complement the advice in the code of practice for residential care, "Home Life". It will give a special emphasis to assessing the quality of care provided and the quality of life of residents as well as physical conditions. Through this national guidance the Department will seek to reduce the variations in standards applied in different areas.

Central Monitoring Arrangements

5.25 The Government intends to strengthen the role of the Department of Health's Social Services Inspectorate in advising and monitoring social services departments on the setting up and operation of their registration and inspection units.

5.26 The Social Services Inspectorate will report to the Secretary of State on:

- the effectiveness of local inspection arrangements;
- the methodologies and standards applied when measuring the quality of services and the quality of care secured.

5.27 These arrangements will complement and enhance existing monitoring systems. The Social Services Inspectorate will retain its current responsibilities for monitoring the quality of management and care provided by social services departments. The Health Advisory Service (HAS) was established in 1969 to visit services for elderly people and people with a mental illness, advise on good practice and report to Ministers. The Department of Health is currently examining the work of the HAS to identify how it might be undertaken effectively following implementation of the proposals in the White Paper "Working for Patients". The National Development Team is available to advise health authorities and social services departments on services for people with a mental handicap and the development of effective strategies. A major current priority is the development of a system of internal and external safeguards to quality. The Audit Commission will maintain its monitoring of the effectiveness of local financial arrangements and conduct selective value for money exercises.

Research

5.28 The community care field is a particularly rich one for research and it has produced impressive work in terms of quality and relevance for both policy makers and service delivery agencies. The Government believes that this successful record of research based innovation will be needed just as much in the future as in the past.

5.29 Many local authorities already contain units with particular responsibilities and the requisite expertise to translate existing research results into material that is directly relevant to their situation. Such units also undertake some research themselves, or commission work from external sources. Often the problems facing one local authority are similar to those of others, and there are valuable examples of local authorities sharing and collaborating to undertake or commission research. The Government welcomes this recognition by local authorities that research can increase the cost-effectiveness of their activities, both through better informed decision making and through the detailed structures and operational systems needed to assess and meet the wide variety of individual needs.

5.30 Centrally the Government, through formal links (for example with the Economic and Social Research Council), and more informally (for example with relevant charities), encourages a collaborative approach to addressing national research needs. The Government draws extensively on a range of contacts both formal and informal with the local authority interests as well as with the research community and the independent sector. This enables the Department of Health's commissioned research programme to be formulated against a wider background knowledge of research activity. In developing priorities for this programe, the Department draws upon established arrangements for seeking the views of representatives of social services managers.

5.31 The proposals set out in this White Paper amount to a significant programme of change and development. The Government believes that research will continue to have an important contribution to make to the effective design and delivery of community cares services. It therefore welcomes this recognition in local authorities, and will itself continue to work with others concerned in defining the key national research issues and designing its own programme of commissioned research in the light of these issues.

CHAPTER SIX: COLLABORATIVE WORKING

CHAPTER SIX: COLLABORATIVE WORKING

6.1 For the past 15 years policies designed to promote effective collaboration between health and local authorities have focused mainly on the mechanics of joint planning and on joint finance. Significant progress has been made but this approach no longer fits well with the Government's aims for the NHS as set out in "Working for Patients", nor with its proposals for community care. The Government recognises that further efforts are needed to improve co-ordination between health and social services. This Chapter sets out the Government's approach for achieving effective joint working, based on strengthened incentives and clearer responsibilities.

The New Context for Collaboration

6.2 The new world in which collaboration will need to take place has a number of key features:

- the Government's plans for reforming the NHS and its proposals for community care will establish an increasingly important distinction between the purchase and provision of health and social care;
- the Government wishes to see responsibility for decisions in the hands of a single, accountable body or person with budgetary responsibility for the expenditure implications of those decisions;
- the Government's approach to the management of both the NHS and of community care is determinedly devolutionary, based on a shift of objective setting and monitoring towards outcomes and away from process.

6.3 These policy developments will substantially strengthen the underlying incentives for health and social services authorities to work closely together:

- the new funding arrangements for residential care mean that discharged hospital patients will have to undergo an assessment of their care needs before the "care" costs of residential accommodation can be met at public expense. Health authorities will therefore need to work with social services authorities to arrange care for elderly people who are inappropriately placed in hospital. At the same time, to make the best use of their "social care" funds, social services authorities will need an effective primary and community health contribution to the development of domiciliary and residential care packages.
- The roles of health and social services authorities as purchasers of services will be more clearly complementary, with both engaged in trying to achieve the best value for public money.

6.4 The Government proposes a fresh approach to collaboration and joint planning by clarifying who does what and redefining joint planning. It will work towards simplifying the statutory framework within which joint planning takes place.

Clarifying who does what

6.5 Successful collaboration requires a clear mutual understanding of each agency's responsibilities and powers, of who decides what, and of how the money flows. This understanding will also help to clarify how and by whom collaboration should be secured.

6.6 The distinction between "health" and "social" care governs the funding of health and social services authorities. Social services authorities will be the "gatekeepers" to social care. There may be areas where the distinction between health and social care is blurred. Health and local authorities will need to decide locally about how they share objectives, responsibilities and funding of different services and, where change is to be made, how it is to be achieved and over what timescale.

6.7 Independent sector service providers will be able to offer both social or health care or a mix of the two. There will be ample scope for the private sector to respond imaginatively to an increased demand for domiciliary based packages of care and for new voluntary and not for profit agencies to offer "mixed" health and social care services. Provided that funding responsibilities are kept separate, there is no reason why health and social services authorities should not sell services and facilities to each other.

6.8 Accountability will match separate funding responsibilities in a way which reinforces the incentives towards collaboration. Service providing agencies will be accountable to buying authorities through contractual agreements. Health authorities will be accountable to the Secretary of State for meeting the health care needs of their resident populations in a cost effective way and will be expected to show that their proposals for community care are shared with local authorities and other agencies. Local authorities will be accountable to their own electorates and will be required to publish their plans for community care services.

Redefining joint planning

6.9 The record of joint planning has been mixed. A modest success can be claimed if judged against realistic criteria but it nevertheless falls short of the aspirations of the mid-1970s. There are three main reasons for reassessing the original objectives of joint planning and its machinery:

- the planning model adopted was derived from the NHS planning system, and was not designed with the financial and political circumstances of local authorities in mind.
- the organisational structure of both health and local authorities will be changed over time by the new purchaser/provider distinction and by the new role for social services authorities as gatekeepers to social care.
- the Government recognises that an insistence in all circumstances on joint plans is no longer appropriate. In future, policy aims must be more closely attuned to the emerging lines of funding and accountability.

6.10 The Government proposes to base future national policy on planning agreements rather than joint plans, although if full joint plans are agreed as the best way forward in particular circumstances there would be no impediment to authorities producing them. These planning agreements would encompass a realistic range of key requirements to be reflected in both health and local authority plans. The key requirements of planning agreements will be:

- common goals derived at least partly from national policy aims for particular client groups;
- funding agreements, setting out the basis on which health and social care will be funded;
- agreed policies on key operational areas, such as quality standards, assessment policies and procedures and discharge policies;
- agreed contract specifications for securing joint working between service providers.

6.11 Such an approach will bring about a shift in focus from means to ends while leaving ample scope for innovation. The Government likewise intends to concentrate on outcomes rather than machinery.

Simplifying the Machinery

6.12 The Government is considering the best way to make changes to Section 22 of the NHS Act 1977 which governs the setting up, membership and operation of Joint Consultative Committees. The purpose of any change, far from signalling a reduced commitment to collaborative working, would be to free health and local authorities to establish the arrangements that most closely fit their own circumstances and methods of working.

The Future of Joint Finance

6.13 Joint finance allocations for 1989/90 stand at £118.5m. Like joint planning it has a mixed record of achievement. Joint finance has provided a real incentive for health and local authorities to work together, in part at least because the money cannot be spent unless both parties agree. And as a mechanism for shifting resources across administrative boundaries, joint finance has pump-primed many valuable and innovative joint social and health care developments. But it does not provide a long-term shift of resources, and many local authorities have found it difficult to enter into the long-term commitments implied.

6.14 The original objectives of joint finance continue to be important to the Government. It remains committed to effecting a shift of resources towards the development of services at and across the boundary between health and social care; and to providing some central stimulus for the development of community care policy locally and in particular for the move away from institutional forms of care. But the new context provided by the Government's proposals for community care means that a reassessment of the part played by joint finance is now needed. The Government will be giving further consideration to its future role in the light of the wider changes.

CHAPTER SEVEN: SERVICES FOR PEOPLE WITH A MENTAL ILLNESS

CHAPTER SEVEN: SERVICES FOR PEOPLE WITH A MENTAL ILLNESS

7.1 The Government recognises the justified concern about the availability of community services for mentally ill people. It is therefore taking three key initiatives, set out later in this chapter, directed at ensuring that both health and social care are provided in ways that give the necessary support.

7.2 Since 1975 it has been the policy of successive Governments to encourage the development of locally-based health and social services, working with the voluntary and private sectors, to meet the needs of people of all ages suffering from mental illness, including those with dementia.

7.3 The main components of a proper locally-based service are:

- provision for children and adolescents with psychological problems. This should be primarily community-based, with easy access to a range of professional support and to hospital services (including in-patient treatment if necessary);

- adequate services for the assessment and treatment of adults whose conditions require short term admission to hospital, and for the longer term treatment, including asylum, of those for whom there is no realistic alternative;

- sufficient places in hospital and local authority hostels, sheltered housing, supported lodgings or other similar forms of provision for adults with a mental illness needing residential care outside hospital, together with an adequate range of day and respite services;

- effective co-ordinated arrangements between health and social services authorities, primary health care teams and voluntary agencies for the continuing health and social care of people with a mental illness living in their own homes or in residential facilities. These should include suitable provision for domiciliary services, support to carers, and the training and education of staff working in the community.

7.4 This policy became possible as research and clinical experience showed that treatment was equally or more effective when less reliance was placed on long term in-patient care and more use made of out-patient, day patient and domiciliary care. Additionally, more effective drug treatments, such as the major tranquillisers which were introduced in the 1950s, transformed the prognosis of the most serious mental illnesses. Where it is effectively implemented, the new style of service offers a much higher quality of life for people with a mental illness and a service more appreciated by their families than is possible in the traditional large and often remote mental hospital. The Government reaffirms its support of the policy as a civilised and humanitarian one.

7.5 Much has been achieved since the 1975 White Paper "Better Services for the Mentally Ill". The Government recognises, however, that progress has not been uniformly satisfactory and there are legitimate concerns that in some places hospital beds have been closed before better, alternative facilities were fully in place. Some reports also suggest that, at times, patients have been discharged without adequate planning to meet their needs in the community. In reaffirming its support for the policy of locally-based services, the Government emphasises that the number of hospital beds should be reduced only as a consequence of the development of new services. Ministers will not approve the closure of any mental hospital unless it can be demonstrated that adequate alternatives have been developed. The procedures outlined in the recent circular "Discharge of Patients from Hospital" (HC(89)5) and the expected statement of good practice from the Royal College of Psychiatrists (see paragraph 7.8 below) should materially improve standards of practice in the discharge of patients.

Health Care

7.6 Two key health care initiatives are proposed to improve the implementation of the Government's policy.

7.7 ***Continuing health care.*** A substantial area of concern over the last few years has been how to make effective arrangements for the continuing care of people being treated in the community. From 1 April 1991 all district health authorities will be required to have instituted, in collaboration with social services authorities, a care programme approach for such people. The essence of this is that the needs of each patient both for continuing health care and social care are assessed before discharge; that effective arrangements are made as to how in principle those needs are to be met, including the maintenance of appropriate registers; and that a named individual is appointed to ensure that they are met in practice.

7.8 The Royal College of Psychiatrists is issuing a preliminary statement of good practice and is developing a more substantive one. As recommended in the Spokes Report (Cm 440), the latter is being undertaken in concert with the other professions involved. The Department of Health will shortly issue guidance to health authorities on care programmes. Taken together, these initiatives offer much clearer guidance on good practice than currently exists.

7.9 The Department of Health is asking Regional Health Authorities to confirm by the end of April 1991 that all District Health Authorities have introduced the care programme approach. The Department will commission research to help evaluate its effectiveness.

7.10 ***Capital for building new facilities.*** Finance from the sale of mental illness and mental handicap hospitals can provide valuable capital for replacement facilities, such as hospital hostels or community units for the elderly mentally ill, but these facilities are needed before hospitals can be vacated. They have to be planned in collaboration with other providing agencies and to compete with other priorities in regional authorities' capital programmes. Thus the whole process may be impeded.

7.11 Existing arrangements for the allocation of capital between and within regions offer one way of addressing this problem. Another possible solution may be for authorities to enter into agreements with developers to build community facilities for those with a mental illness, in return for which the developers would receive all or part of the vacated sites.

7.12 The Department of Health is therefore inviting Regional Health Authorities to identify sites where partnership with the private sector could enable earlier and orderly progress to be made in putting new forms of service in place. The aim will be to bring about the degree of private sector involvement that can be demonstrated to maximise value for money.

Social Care

7.13 The Government's third initiative relates to the ***provision of social care***. Consistent with its general approach, the Government agrees with Sir Roy Griffiths' recommendation that social services authorities should continue to be responsible for providing social care to those with a mental illness who require it.

7.14 In the face of other calls on resources, local authorities generally have not been able to give as much priority to providing services to those with a mental illness as other vulnerable groups. It is not possible to give an exact figure but the Department of Health judges that possibly only about 3% of social services authorities' expenditure is currently spent on services specifically for those with a mental illness. The level of service provision available varies considerably between authorities.

7.15 To increase the social care available for people with a mental illness the Government proposes to make a specific grant to social services authorities from 1991/92. The Government will be issuing separate guidance on the size, distribution and monitoring of the grant in due course.

7.16 In order to encourage the joint planning of services, and proper collaboration in relation to care programmes, the Government will make this grant payable through Regional Health Authorities as the agents of the Secretary of State for Health, on the basis of plans for the development of social care agreed between social services authorities and the matching district health authorities.

7.17 In the light of the above proposals in relation to the continuing health and social care of those with a mental illness, the Government does not intend to implement Section 7 of the Disabled Persons (Services, Consultation and Representation) Act 1986, which would impose statutory obligations on health and social services authorities in respect of those leaving hospital after six months or more as in-patients. The need to implement Section 7 will be reconsidered in the light of several years' experience of the introduction of care programmes and the response to the specific grant.

Other Initiatives

7.18 In addition to the three key initiatives set out above, the Department of Health has work well advanced or planned in the following areas, all of which will support health and social services authorities in making effective arrangements for the treatment and care of those with a mental illness.

7.19 ***Guidance on compulsory admission to hospital.*** A minority of those suffering from a mental disorder pose such a threat to themselves or others that they need to be admitted to hospital compulsorily under the provisions of the Mental Health Act 1983. There seems to be wide agreement that the provisions of the Act are satisfactory, but some concern that its interpretation by practitioners is sometimes not. The Code of Practice required under the Act will be laid before Parliament shortly.

7.20 ***The contribution of the voluntary sector.*** The voluntary sector makes a major contribution to the services available to those with a mental illness, their carers and relatives in all parts of the country. The Department of Health has a key role in encouraging the development of an active and innovative voluntary sector by central funding; current support to voluntary organisations in the mental health area (including mental handicap) is at the level of about £2.4m a year. To ensure that the £2.4m is spent in a way that best supports sufferers, their carers and relatives, the Department is reviewing its funding strategy, and hopes to further the development of a wide and innovatory range of voluntary services.

7.21 ***Prevention and detection of mental illness.*** The Department of Health is sponsoring a series of conferences about mental illness and the primary care services, with a view to identifying ways of improving prevention, detection and management by the primary care team. A report arising from the conferences will be published next year and promising approaches will be developed further.

7.22 ***Mental illness among the homeless population.*** The incidence of mental illness among homeless and destitute men and women in London and other cities has been linked by some to the fall in the number of hospital beds. Projects funded by the Department of Health have shown that, most commonly, homeless mentally ill people have had care organised outside hospital but have lost touch with services. In future, the numbers losing touch should fall as a result of the introduction of the care programme approach, but there is a sizeable current problem of sufferers not receiving treatment. The Department of Health is exploring what practical steps can be taken to assist such people to obtain the help they need.

7.23 ***Emergency care for those with mental illness.*** Concern has been expressed about the adequacy of arrangements at local level for the emergency care of people suffering from mental illness. In some places this need is met through the normal accident and emergency arrangements; in others by specialist mental health emergency arrangements. The Department of Health intends to commission research to establish the extent of current arrangements and to help evaluate alternative forms.

CHAPTER EIGHT: RESOURCES FOR COMMUNITY CARE

CHAPTER EIGHT: RESOURCES FOR COMMUNITY CARE

8.1 The past decade has seen considerable expansion in expenditure on community care, resulting in significant growth in the volume of services provided. This Chapter sets out the Government's record of investment in community care and its proposals for ensuring that in future all available resources are put to best possible use. The implications of the Government's plans for that most important of all resources - the workforce - are also considered.

Growth in Expenditure on Community Care

8.2 Both central and local government have given priority to expenditure on community care and their record is impressive. In Great Britain in 1979/80 gross current expenditure on core community care services (not including administration or joint finance) was £1,169m. By 1987/88 this had risen to £3,444m - an increase of 68% in real terms. Table 1 shows the breakdown of expenditure by agency.

8.3 At the beginning of the decade the bulk of these services was provided by local authorities (Chart 1). Their expenditure was met through unhypothecated central government grants, local rates and income from charges. Some 55% of local authority gross expenditure was on residential care for elderly people, younger disabled people, mentally handicapped children and adults, and mentally ill people, with 45% on domiciliary services. By 1987/88 the local authority gross expenditure was more evenly balanced with slightly over 50% on residential care and just under 50% on community based services, especially home helps, day care centres, meals services and adult training centres (Chart 2 and Table 1). Charges have remained an important source of income for local authorities. In 1987/88 charges raised over £360m from residential care and nearly £80m from domiciliary care. Allowing for charges shifts the balance of local authority net expenditure firmly towards domiciliary care.

8.4 Across all client groups local authority personal social services net expenditure has grown by 37% in real terms during the whole decade up to 1989/90. Gross expenditure on community health services for health aspects of community care has grown by 35% in real terms up to 1987/88. The largest item is the district nursing service, but expenditure on chiropody and health visiting is also significant (Table 1). The overall growth in resources has been more than enough to keep up with the demographic pressures considered later in this Chapter.

8.5 It is, however, well known that the expansion of local authority and community health based services has been outstripped by the growth in social security payments to people in independent sector residential and nursing homes. Social security expenditure on independent residential and nursing home care rose in cash terms from £10m in December 1979 to over £1,000m by May 1989. Chart 3 shows this growth in real terms. However, only part of this sum goes to meet care costs, and only a small proportion of this in 1991/92 would be spent on the new residents for whom local authorities will then become responsible (see 8.23 below).

8.6 The rapid growth in social security expenditure has contributed to a rise in real terms of 96% in total spending on residential care across all sectors between 1979/80 and 1987/88 whereas total spending on domiciliary services has risen in real terms by 41%. (Chart 2).

8.7 The social security system also makes an important contribution to community care through expenditure on a number of benefits for those needing care and their carers, in particular Attendance Allowance and Invalid Care Allowance. Spending on these two benefits alone has risen from £205m in 1979/80 to £1,081m in 1987/88.

Growth of Community Care Services

8.8 The Government's investment in community care has led to a considerable expansion in the volume of community services provided. Between 1979/80 and 1987/88 the number of places in local authority and registered residential homes in England rose by 47% to 302,600, most of the increase being in private homes, while the number of beds in private nursing homes more than doubled to 68,900. Over the same period, in England, staff of local authority home help services increased by 27% to a whole time equivalent of 59,500 and the number of elderly people treated by the district nursing service rose by 24% to 1.6 million.

8.9 There has also been a significant change in the settings in which care is delivered. Large numbers of people have moved out of hospital into community settings. In England between 1979/80 and 1986/87, the number of available beds in NHS mental handicap hospitals and units fell by 13,100 to 36,300, while places in residential homes and NHS community units for people with a mental handicap rose by 13,900 to 29,700. In addition, adult training centre places for people with a mental handicap rose by 9,400 to 51,700. Over the same period, around 6,000 people were discharged from mental illness hospitals and units after a stay of 5 years or more, while the number of first attendances by day patients at NHS day care facilities increased by 18,000 to 59,000 per year, the number of local authority day centre places for mentally ill people increased by almost a thousand to 5,900 and 3,300 more places were made available in all residential homes, bringing the total to 9,200.

Demographic Pressures

8.10 Most people needing community care are elderly and there is an increasing tendency for elderly people to live alone. The number of people aged 65 and over is projected to rise from 8.4 million in 1985 to 9.0 million by 2001. Chart 4 provides a graphic illustration of this trend. Growth will be greatest amongst the very elderly who are also most likely to be disabled and in greater need of community care. The numbers of people aged over 85 are projected to rise from 695,000 in 1986 to 1,146,000 in 2001. The OPCS disability survey showed that there were about three quarters of a million severely disabled adults aged 65 and over living in the community in 1986. On current projections there will be just under 900,000 such people by 2001. (Chart 5). These demographic trends are already taken account of, and will continue to be allowed for, in the Government's consideration of its grant to local authorities.

8.11 Previous chapters have acknowledged the major contribution of private carers. The 1985 OPCS study of informal carers identified around 6 million carers in Great Britain, of whom 3.7 million carried the main care responsibility and 1.4 million devoted at least twenty hours a week to caring. Their total input was greater than the combined inputs financed from central and local government. The Government recognises that demographic trends will have implications for the future availability of carers.

The Government's Proposals for Funding Residential and Nursing Home Care

8.12 The Government's proposals for reforming the funding of residential and nursing home care are set out below. They are intended to ensure that people enter homes only when a proper assessment of their needs has established that this is the right form of care for them within available resources and that residential care and nursing homes take their proper place within the spectrum of community care provision.

The Effects of Social Security Payments

8.13 Special arrangements for social security benefits, principally Income Support, apply at present to residents of most independent residential care and nursing homes. The arrangements embrace all homes registered under the Registered Homes Act 1984, together with a small number of others, such as those run by the Abbeyfield Society or by organisations established by Royal Charter or Act of Parliament. Residential Care Homes with less than four residents, which are not registerable under the Act, can also be included provided they meet certain criteria which enable social security adjudication officers to establish that the care provided is similar to that in registered homes.

8.14 At present, Income Support is available to people on low incomes to help with the home's fees and the cost of any extra meals not included in the charge. A separate personal expenses allowance is provided. Housing benefit is generally not available. The amount which can be paid towards fees is subject to an overall maximum, known as the "limit". The limits vary according to whether the home is a residential care home or nursing home, and the type of care provided. Higher limits apply in Greater London. Because Income Support provides help with accommodation and care costs as well as living costs, an individual claiming in a home obtains substantially higher benefit than someone outside a home claiming the normal Income Support personal allowances and premiums.

8.15 These arrangements have undoubtedly been of very real value to large numbers of vulnerable people and their families, and they have been the channel through which very significant public resources have been shifted into the provision of community care. However, as earlier Chapters have made clear, they have serious drawbacks. Their unintended consequence has been that priority has not been given to developing services to enable people to be supported in their own homes, with a consequent restriction on the choice available to individuals, their families and the professional care services.

8.16 The social security system also does not readily permit any assessment of whether its payments are value for money. Adjudication officers have neither the duty nor the expertise to determine whether the charges met from Income Support are reasonable for the level and quality of care provided. The new system which the Government is proposing will enable account to be taken of variations in the costs of running homes in different parts of the country.

The New Funding System

8.17 The Government proposes to introduce a single unified budget to cover the costs of social care, whether in a person's own home or in a residential care or nursing home. The new budget will include the care element of social security payments to people in private and voluntary residential care and nursing homes. Local authorities are to be given responsibility for managing this budget and making best use of funds available in the light of an assessment of an individual's needs. Collaboration between medical, nursing and social services agencies will be essential, particularly when assessing need for nursing home care.

8.18 Consequential changes will be needed to the way in which Income Support is paid to people in residential care and nursing homes. People who enter homes under the new funding structure and who need public financial support will no longer have their care costs met by social security. In place of the special limits they will be able to claim help from the normal Income Support system of personal allowances and premiums, and from Housing Benefit. They will receive assistance on the same basis as that which they could obtain in their own homes. The financial incentive towards residential care under present Income Support rules will therefore be eliminated. Other than any necessary adjustments to the Housing Benefit entitlement, the sources of income from the benefit system will remain the same when a person enters or leaves a private or voluntary residential setting. This is the approach that has already been adopted for people in board and lodging and hostel accommodation who are claiming Income Support. Most significantly, it allows Housing Benefit payments to be determined in the light of local conditions. For this reason, and to maintain consistency for both claimants and social security offices, the Government has decided in favour of this arrangement rather than the new residential allowance suggested by Sir Roy Griffiths.

8.19 The Government recognises the importance of keeping funding arrangements as straightforward as possible for individual residents. It has therefore decided that local authorities should be responsible for meeting the cost of places in residential or nursing home care, requiring residents to pay over a part of their income from social security benefits. The Government is giving further consideration to how these arrangements will operate in practice.

8.20 Under the new arrangements local housing authorities will have to determine what constitutes the "eligible rent" on which Housing Benefit can be paid. The Government will bring forward proposals on the method to be used, and will be consulting the Local Authority Associations on the details.

8.21 The Government intends to introduce these changes from 1 April 1991. In order to secure a smooth transition to the new funding structure, the new arrangements for social security benefit will apply only to people who become resident in registered residential care homes or nursing homes on or after that date. Chapter 9 sets out the arrangements for people who are already resident in homes before April 1991.

Funding for Local Authorities

8.22 Chapter 3 has set out the Government's proposals for the new role and responsibilities of local authorities. The Government recognises that local authorities will need adequate resources to enable them to discharge their new responsibilities including assessment, case management and enabling the provision of appropriate care. The Government will transfer to local authorities the resources which it would have otherwise provided to finance care through social security payments to people in residential and nursing homes.

8.23 Calculation of the sums to be transferred will take account of four factors:

- the Income Support that would have been payable under the present scheme;
- the normal Income Support and Housing Benefit that will be payable to new residents;
- the continuing commitment to those residents with preserved rights to the current scheme;
- the rate at which local authorities will assume responsibility for the care of new clients. Account will be taken both of the natural demographic turnover of cases and the overall growth due to demographic and other factors.

8.24 The transfer of funds will thus be phased to reflect the declining proportion of residents in independent homes previously eligible for income support who continue to be supported entirely by social security. The best estimate presently available would suggest that approximately one fifth of the eventual total (as determined in 8.23) will be transferred in the first year (This is illustrated in Chart 6). This will need to be kept under review as detailed information becomes available. The gradual switch of resources will ensure a smooth transition to the new structure and enable local authorities to build up their support as the numbers of people requiring assessment increase. The transfer will also include an allowance for the changes in payment of Attendance Allowance (detailed in 9.8). The aggregate amount of the transferred resources will allow for the projected growth in the numbers of people needing support. Final decisions on resource issues will be taken in next year's Public Expenditure Survey following discussions with the Local Authority Associations.

How Will Funds be Paid to Local Authorities?

8.25 The additional provision for local authorities will be distributed through the Revenue Support Grant. The Government gave careful consideration to Sir Roy Griffiths' case for a specific grant but concluded that a large scale specific grant is not necessary to secure community care objectives. Support for community care expenditure, as with other important local authority functions, would be best provided principally through the Revenue Support Grant. This will ensure maximum local accountability and encourage value for money by enabling local authorities to make their own decisions about community care, based on knowledge of local factors. Chart 7 shows the anticipated sources of local authority funds for community care.

8.26 The Government has decided to create a specific grant to encourage the development of social care for people with a mental illness to be paid via health authorities.

The Distribution of Funds

8.27 Government support for community care expenditure for local authorities will be distributed through the Revenue Support Grant in the normal way by taking account of the Standard Spending Assessment for the Personal Social Services. Details of how this will operate will be discussed with the Local Authority Associations. The Standing Spending Assessment formula will continue to take account of the amount of expenditure appropriate for local authorities to incur on supported community care services, including authorities' increasing responsibility for clients who would previously have been funded through social security payments. The phasing of the additional funding will need to be considered.

Health Authority Funding

8.28 Health authorities will continue to fund mainstream community care activity from within their overall allocation of resources.

8.29 The Government considered Sir Roy Griffiths' proposal that health authority spending on community care should be ring-fenced. It concluded, however, that attempting to do so would carry too great a risk of distorting future spending in this area. The growth of community care will depend crucially on the availability and growth of community-based alternatives to care in long-stay institutions. Setting aside a fixed sum for this purpose will not provide the flexibility which will be needed to respond to this diversity of opportunity. Community health services will play an important part in enabling people to live in the community, although it is not possible to say what proportion of in-patients may, in future, be supported outside hospital, nor what proportion of, for example, district nursing or health visiting comes within community care for these groups.

The Social Services Workforce

8.30 The provision of social care services is a labour intensive activity. In taking on their new responsibilities, social services staff will be building on existing skills and competencies, but their training will need to reflect their new roles.

8.31 The social services workforce is very diverse, with staff operating at vocational, professional and managerial levels. In England, it consists of over 232,000 whole time equivalent employees (at September 1987), including 27,000 social workers,and has grown by almost 25% over the last decade. Many of these staff are involved primarily in child care services.

8.32 The proposals in this White Paper will have implications for the roles of all staff involved in community care, including:

- 5,500 senior management and planning staff
- 25,000 staff with assessment and case management responsibilities
- 12,000 other middle and first line managers, mainly in care establishments.
- 115,000 staff involved in the direct delivery of care and support.

There will also be implications for staff working in the independent sector, including private, not for profit, and voluntary organisations which the Government expects to see playing a larger role in the provision of community care.

8.33 It will be important to continue to develop multi-disciplinary training for staff in all caring professions, including the provision of joint training at both the qualifying and post-qualifying stages.

New Ways of Working

8.34 The Government recognises that its proposals will have an impact on the ways in which managers and staff at all levels of the social services workforce carry out their work. The implementation of a case management approach will require social workers to develop and apply their professional assessment and counselling skills at the same time as exercising some resource management responsibilities. Whatever the professional or occupational background of case managers, they will need to continue to have available to them staff with training, skills and qualifications in social work and occupational therapy.

8.35 The contribution of vocational staff providing social care will become increasingly important. As an increasing number of more dependent people are supported in the community there will be a need for the provision of more personal care by home care workers. The Government welcomes the new developments in the role of home care workers which are already underway in a number of areas and therefore does not think it necessary to create a new occupation of "community carer" to carry out basic tasks of personal and social care.

8.36 Social services authorities will need to review their training strategies for all sections of their workforce. Such strategies should include provision, within available resources, for the training of managers at all levels in skills such as defining service specifications, managing new contractual relationships with service providers and financial management.

Initiatives to Improve Training

8.37 The Government has already recognised the importance of increasing training opportunities for staff working in the personal social services. In co-operation with the Central Council for Education and Training in Social Work (CCETSW), the Local Authority Associations, the Local Government Training Board (LGTB), and other interested organisations, it is developing a balanced programme of training improvements which will assist with the implementation of the policies set out in this White Paper.

8.38 Steps have already been taken to improve the provision of management training. The Department of Health has funded work by the LGTB on management development. In preparation for the increased responsibilities of local social services authorities for the planning and management of community care, alongside their substantial responsibilities for child care and protection, the Government is introducing in 1990/91 a Training Support Programme of £2 million for training in social services management. The details of this programme will be discussed with the Local Authority Associations.

8.39 It is essential that qualifying training for social workers equips them to operate effectively in their new roles. CCETSW is introducing a new Diploma in Social Work (DipSW) to replace the existing CQSW and CSS awards.

8.40 The Department of Health and CCETSW are seeking to establish increased opportunities for post-qualifying training. The Department of Health has convened a working group, which includes representatives of employer and training organisations to consider these issues. The Department of Health's Training Support Programmes enable local authorities to increase the opportunities available to their staff for pursuit of post-qualifying level training.

8.41 Major improvements are also underway in social care training for social services staff. Social care staff at vocational levels constitute by far the majority of the community care workforce, including 60,000 staff in domiciliary services and 68,000 staff working in residential services for adults. The quality of services for community care consumers is dependent on the skills of these staff. In the past however, their training needs have not generally been well met. In order to address these shortcomings, the Government set up the National Council for Vocational Qualifications in 1986 to establish a system of national vocational qualifications (NVQ). A consortium of interests (the Care Sector Consortium) representing employers and staff from the statutory and independent sectors are working to secure a recognised pattern of vocational qualifications and training for all those working in the care sector. Their further work on the NVQ will take account of the Government's proposal for community care.

8.42 The Department of Health's Training Support Programme for staff working with elderly people has made an important contribution to the training of local authority social care staff. In 1988/89, the first year of the programme's operation, local authorities planned to provide training opportunities under the programme for approximately 70,000 staff working at vocational levels, making effective use of £10 million expenditure, 70% of which was in the form of a specific grant managed by the Department of Health. This programme will continue in 1990/91 to assist social services authorities to train their workforces in preparation for an extended role in community care for elderly people.

CHAPTER NINE: HELP FROM SOCIAL SECURITY

CHAPTER NINE: HELP FROM SOCIAL SECURITY

9.1 Chapter 8 has outlined the main changes proposed to the way in which social security will be paid to people in independent residential care and nursing homes when the new funding structure is in place. This chapter sets out the Government's proposals for paying benefits to people who are already in homes when the new arrangements come into effect and describes the effects of the new structure on residents' entitlement to social security benefits other than Income Support. Social Fund Community Care Grants will continue to complement the social care responsibilities of the local authorities, and the Government will also continue to seek ways to build on the constructive arrangements recently agreed with the Local Authority Associations to improve co-operation between DSS local offices and social services/work departments.

Preserved Rights for Existing Residents

9.2 The Government intends to preserve the present scheme of special Income Support limits for existing claimants who are in residential care and nursing homes when the new funding structure is introduced on 1 April 1991. The right to claim Income Support under the preserved scheme will also be safeguarded for residents supporting themselves at that date but who may have recourse subsequently to public financial support.

9.3 Access to the preserved scheme will be given if, on 31 March 1991 (the day before the change to the benefit arrangements), a resident or claimant is, or would normally be, living in a residential care or nursing home where the Income Support limits apply. Income Support will continue for claimants, including existing residents who subsequently become claimants, whose entitlement in a home is not interrupted. Entitlement will not be affected by a claimant or resident moving home or, in most circumstances , leaving a home altogether for long periods: to go into hospital, for example.

9.4 These rules will apply to the residents of all registered homes and to the residents of those homes which are not registerable but are specially catered for in the present Income Support scheme - such as homes run by the Abbeyfield Society or under Royal Charter. Income Support claimants in "small homes" - unregistered homes with fewer than four residents - who are claiming Income Support on 31 March 1991 as if resident in a registered home, will have access to preserved Income Support in exactly the same way as other claimants. However, other residents of small homes who are not claiming Income Support as if resident in a registered home will not have access to preserved Income Support.

Respite Care

9.5 Respite Care is the term used to describe an arrangement whereby elderly or disabled people, normally cared for at home by relatives, are placed temporarily in alternative accommodation to give their usual carers a break. Respite Care is most commonly provided by the NHS, by Local Authorities in their own accommodation and in independent residential care and nursing homes. Local authorities and voluntary organisations also support a range of schemes in less formal care environments. The funding of respite care is affected by the new arrangements only in so far as it is currently provided through Income Support. Future arrangements for funding respite care need to reflect the primary responsibility of Local Authorities in facilitating and funding it as part of a package of care. The existing rules which preclude the payment of Housing Benefit to meet the accommodation costs of admission to respite care will be retained. However, the transfer of resources made to Local Authorities after April 1991 will take into account their responsibility for this developing area.

Attendance Allowance

9.6 Attendance Allowance is a non-means tested benefit paid to severely disabled people who need a great deal of support. It is paid at two rates, one for people who have attendance needs by day or night, and a higher amount for people with attendance needs day and night. Together with the associated Invalid Care Allowance, it is an important part of the social security support for community care.

9.7 The proposed changes in funding community care will not alter the present arrangements for paying Attendance Allowance to people in private households, or to people who go into independent residential or nursing homes without any other assistance from public funds (other than state benefits). The transfer to local authorities of responsibility for assisting with the care costs of residents in independent homes will however require a change in the current rules intended to prevent double provision.

9.8 At present, Attendance Allowance is offset against any Income Support paid to residents in independent homes and is not paid at all to residents in local authority and other publicly funded accommodation. This is to avoid double provision. For people in independent homes with preserved rights to Income Support, the position on or after 1 April 1991 will be the same as it is now.

9.9 However, Attendance Allowance will not be paid to residents in independent homes who from 1 April 1991 will be assisted by the local authority. This new rule will make no difference to the residents concerned, nor will it remove any continuing, underlying entitlement to Attendance Allowance. It will, however, put such local authority assisted independent care on the same footing as other publicly funded accommodation. Any underlying entitlement to Attendance Allowance established before or during any period of local authority assisted residence and still in force when that period stops can be activated once that period stops, and Attendance Allowance then paid immediately in the normal way.

Independent Living Fund.

9.10 There would clearly be an overlap between the Independent Living Fund and the intended responsibilities of local authorities which will need to be reviewed.

CHAPTER TEN: COMMUNITY CARE IN SCOTLAND

CHAPTER TEN: COMMUNITY CARE IN SCOTLAND

10.1 The aim of community care in Scotland is to enable those who need care to live as independently as possible in their own homes or elsewhere in the community and to reduce current reliance on residential care. The development of community care is a well established objective of health and social care policy and substantial resources are already devoted to the provision of community services. The broad policy objectives for community care are outlined in Scottish Health Authorities Review of Priorities for the Eighties and Nineties (SHARPEN) and the Secretary of State continues to endorse these policies. However, more needs to be done. In Scotland the aims now are: to redefine and clarify the responsibilities of the agencies concerned with care; to develop services that allow for a range of options for those in need of care; and to ensure that residential care is used appropriately. The key objectives and changes set out in Chapter 1 apply equally to Scotland.

Present Position

10.2 The Government's proposals build on the progress that has been made by Scottish local authorities and Health Boards. They have developed jointly and separately a range of services and facilities which has helped in shifting the emphasis from institutional care to domiciliary and other community-based services. Between 1979-80 and 1988-89 expenditure on the community health services in Scotland rose by 43% in real terms and provision for social work services generally by 53%. Between 1979 and 1987 the number of people with mental handicap in hospitals fell by 21% while day care provision for this group rose by 39%. The number of long-stay mentally ill hospital patients fell by 13%. Between 1979 and 1988 the number of clients of the home help service rose by 35% and day centre places for elderly people rose by 92%. Places in residential homes for people with mental handicap increased by 73% and for the elderly by 21%.

10.3 In parallel with these developments, there have since 1979 been significant increases in Scotland in the provision of all forms of special needs housing. This provision has ranged from housing with minor adaptations, largely indistinguishable from other housing, through specially designed sheltered housing developments, to small hostel accommodation catering for groups of 8 to 12 people. In the public sector, the number of sheltered dwellings increased from 7,000 in 1979 to 25,000 in 1988 - an almost four fold increase. Private sector sheltered housing developments have added significantly to this total (although comprehensive statistics are not available). The number of amenity dwellings has risen from 3,100 in 1979 to 11,600 in 1988 and housing for disabled people has grown from 3,000 to 15,900 dwellings over the same period. Increasing efforts are also being made to enable more people to stay longer in their own homes, for example through care and repair schemes at both national and local level run by voluntary bodies and local authorities. The Government also proposes to clarify the powers of local authorities and the Secretary of State in Scotland to offer financial assistance to organisations providing services for owners or occupiers in arranging or encouraging the carrying out of works to their homes.

New Role for Local Authorities

10.4 Under the Government's proposals to secure the development of a wider range of community care services local authorities in Scotland (that is regional and islands councils as well as social work authorities) will assume new responsibilities which will require statutory changes. Local authorities are likely to remain for the time being major providers of care facilities and they will retain their existing functions in relation to their own residential provision but will be expected to move towards an enabling role rather than that of direct provider. The Government would thus wish them to promote and make greater use of the facilities of the voluntary and private sector, taking account of the different circumstances in different areas of Scotland.

10.5 Scottish local authorities will be responsible in future for carrying out assessments of people for whom individual care programmes may be required, whether domiciliary or residential. The assessment procedure will involve health professionals and other agencies as necessary, will take account of the individual's views and, where appropriate, those of informal carers. The principles to be adopted in the conduct of assessments are set out in Chapter 3 and the Scottish Office will be issuing a detailed Code of Guidance, following discussion with interested bodies.

10.6 Where the assessment suggests that an individual's needs may be better met in a non-residential setting, the authority will, in co-operation with the Health Board and other agencies as necessary, devise a package of care within available resources in line with the outcome of the assessment. The aim of such a package will be to help support the individual in his or her own home or elsewhere in the community for as long as possible. Where the assessment concludes that placement in a residential or nursing home is more appropriate, the authority will be able to provide accommodation in one of their own residential homes, as at present, or, under new powers, make continuing payments towards the costs of accommodation in other homes, in so far as these costs are not met from income support and housing benefit. The financial arrangements for local authorities' own residential homes are dealt with in Chapter 3.

Community Care Plans

10.7 The Government wishes to strengthen public accountability for the delivery of community care. Local authorities will be required to prepare clear plans in conjunction with Health Boards, housing authorities, voluntary agencies including housing associations and the private sector which define objectives and targets and describe procedures for monitoring progress towards the achievement of effective community care. The general principles which will apply are set out in Chapter 5. Local authorities will be consulted in drawing up guidance on the form and content of the plans. There will also be discussions on all aspects of the new arrangements and in particular how they will relate to the existing planning system.

10.8 The community care plans should cover a three year period and include targets for the development of local authorities' own services as well as details of local authority proposals for purchasing services from the voluntary and private sector; proposals for individual case management; for developing a range of services; and for handling comments and complaints. Community care plans should be public documents and should be produced in a format which takes this into account.

10.9 Scottish local authorities will be required to prepare such plans by 1 April 1991. It is proposed to take powers to enable the Secretary of State to issue directions, to call for reports from authorities or otherwise enquire into and examine any aspect of community care services in their areas.

Registration and Inspection of Residential Homes

10.10 At present local authorities exercise statutory responsibilities for registration and inspection of residential establishments in the private and voluntary sectors. This responsibility under the Social Work (Scotland) Act 1968 will remain with local authorities. In exercising these responsibilities local authorities need to adopt an even-handed approach in setting the standards for registration of premises in all sectors.

10.11 It is therefore proposed that local authorities in Scotland should set up arm's length inspection units to carry out the statutory inspection of voluntary and private homes and comparable inspections of local authorities' own homes. Unit staff would be appointed by the local authority but would work separately from the operational management of the social work department and report direct to the Director of Social Work. The local authority would be expected to secure the involvement of the private and voluntary sectors in the processes, procedures and standards adopted in the inspection process. Arrangements should also be made for taking the views of residents into account. A consultative document will be issued shortly setting out in more detail how the units should be set up and operate in Scotland, their line of accountability within the local authorities and possible ways of involving the voluntary and private sector in the inspection process.

Social Work Staff

10.12 Development of community care services in Scotland will affect the professional and vocational roles of a wide range of staff in the statutory, private and voluntary sectors. In taking on their new responsibilities social work staff will be building on existing skills but their training will need to reflect their new roles in developing local authority community care plans, in procuring and commissioning services and in implementing individual care programmes with professional and financial oversight.

10.13 In Scotland the Government will continue to support the Central Council for Education and Training in Social Work, and other interests, in work to enhance the quality of professional and vocational training for staff in social work agencies. For post qualifying training the Government has decided to commission a central training programme in Scotland for a number of key staff from statutory and non-statutory social work agencies who will be well placed to influence the planning and provision of services. This Scottish programme will enhance the quality of training in community care and act as a catalyst for other developments within agencies and educational institutions. Grants of up to £80,000 per annum over three years (with possible extension to five) will be offered to meet core programme costs. In addition the Government will discuss further training issues with relevant interests.

Health Boards and Community Care

10.14 Health Boards are already involved with local authorities in jointly planning community services. This valuable joint working needs to continue. The enhanced role of local authorities for community care does not reduce in any way the part to be played by the National Health Service in taking forward community care objectives. Indeed, it is even more important that Health Boards should work and plan closely with local authorities and the voluntary and private sectors in the provision of facilities in the community.

10.15 The primary care and hospital sectors are both already extensively involved in helping people in need to stay in or return to their own homes or local communities. At present general practitioners and other health care professionals (hospital social workers, health visitors, and district nursing, community psychiatric and school nursing staff) play a central role in identifying an individual's need for community or residential care. General practitioners are invariably involved in assessment for the suitability of residential care. In future general practitioners and other medical professionals should be more involved in assessment procedures with local authority staff for the wider spectrum of community care provision. This will require improved links between the general practitioner, the primary health care team and social work departments. The Scottish Office will discuss with the Health Boards, local authorities and the professions how this can best be done. They will be asked in particular to examine whether lines of communication are clear between general practice and social work and if not whether better locally agreed arrangements could be introduced which would take account of such difficulties as the variation in catchment areas.

10.16 Separate consideration will be given to the role of the general practitioner in relation to the new assessment procedures. There will be consultation on the detailed arrangements required. The role of individual general practitioners and medical specialists, such as geriatricians and psychiatrists, in these procedures may be reviewed and particularly their links with other health and social work professionals in the community services who will also have a role to play in assessment.

10.17 Health Boards will be asked to draw up their own plans which will be agreed with local authorities and other interested parties for the development of community care in their area. These plans will require to be submitted to the Scottish Office and progress will be monitored as part of the Accountability Review (part of the monitoring arrangements of the Scottish Home and Health Department) to ensure that adequate funds are being devoted to this. It is not expected that this will represent a net extra burden upon Health Boards who should be able within their overall planning responsibilities to highlight those features of forward planning directly relevant to the new framework for community care arising from the Government's proposals. There will be a need for planning agreements between local authorities and Health Boards setting out shared assumptions and objectives as the basis of the community care plans of the Health Boards and the local authorities. The details will be the subject of further consultations.

Priorities for Client Groups

10.18 The main groups requiring care have different needs and priorities. It is acknowledged that the bulk of care of people with disabilities, including those with considerable disabilities, falls on family, friends and neighbours. The role of the informal carer is vital. These informal carers require help and respite, and support will therefore require to be made available on a flexible basis to suit a wide variety of needs. In all these fields the voluntary sector has much to offer.

Elderly People

10.19 In Scotland there are 757,000 persons over 65 years of age. This figure will increase by about 4.6% by 2001, with the steepest increase in those over 85. Particular regard will need to be paid to the mental health of the elderly, given the ageing population and the likelihood of an increasing number of people suffering from dementia. The objective for elderly people is to provide services and facilities which will enable them to continue to live in the community for as long as possible, if it is their wish to do so.

10.20 Local authorities should give special emphasis to the development of domiciliary and day care services as an alternative to residential care, which may be provided by themselves or the private and voluntary sectors, aimed at supporting informal carers such as family, neighbours and friends.

10.21 The Government is keen to develop a more flexible use of residential care for elderly people including a wider use of respite care. Admission to residential care for periods of respite, in conjunction with the use of day care facilities, may be part of a package of care which could help reduce the need for long-term residential provision. Admission to residential care on a long-term basis should only be made after careful assessment has established that this is the best course of action.

People with Physical Disability

10.22 For those with a physical disability the priority is the development of services which will enable more independent living. An important basis for this is well planned joint working among the various agencies concerned. A number of reports, including the recent Scottish Health Services Planning Council Report on Services for Young Physically Disabled Adults in Scotland, have recommended the establishment of joint care planning groups to design co-ordinated services and where necessary re-allocate resources. The promotion of independent living requires providers of services to be well-informed. There will be a need to improve the design and co-ordination of specialist support services, including a combination of respite, day care, domiciliary care and rehabilitation with a more varied system of support for those with a disability and their carers. These changes should take into account the present level of dependence on occupational therapists as the main service providers for people with a physical disability and allow better use of their skills.

People with a Mental Handicap

10.23 People with a mental handicap have various special needs concerned with personal and social support, health care, further education and employment opportunities. Included in this group are those people who in addition to their mental handicap have other specific needs and disabilities, such as physical handicap or mental illness. To ensure appropriate community care for this wide-ranging group close collaboration between local authorities, Health Boards and other agencies will remain essential.

10.24 The results of a major study in Scotland published in 1987 suggested that more than 90% of residents in mental handicap hospitals would be capable of being accommodated in the community depending on the availability of suitable accommodation and personal support. The move out of institutional settings is a central feature of the Government's social policy. Increased resources have already been made available to improve accommodation and services in mental handicap hospitals. The number of long-stay residents in these hospitals has steadily decreased during the last 10 years as new admissions have been curtailed and many existing patients have successfully taken up residence in the community. The Government's policy is to continue this process and provide opportunities for people with a mental handicap to join in the life of the community to the fullest extent possible.

People with Mental Illness

10.25 For people with mental illness, including those with dementia, the Government's aim is that care should be provided to allow them to live in the community wherever this is possible. Health Boards and local authorities already collaborate on the care of people with mental illness and recognise the importance of liaison particularly in notification to local authorities of Health

Boards' intentions regarding discharge of patients with serious and longer term mental health problems from hospital. This liaison is crucial in identifying suitable support services in the community which can help restrict unnecessary re-admission to hospital and enhance the prospects for independent living for this group.

10.26 The Government has, however, considered whether more can be done to develop the quality of collaboration between authorities in the specific case of patients due to be discharged from hospitals for the mentally ill. The Government considers that because of the importance in this area of securing full co-ordination of health and social work services there are grounds for introducing more formal arrangements than apply at present. Health Boards and local authorities will receive guidance to prepare joint care programmes for individuals with long-term illnesses due to be discharged from these hospitals. Health Boards and local authorities will also, from their respective viewpoints, complete an assessment of the health and social care needs for each individual before discharge takes place.

10.27 The Government does not propose to prescribe in detail the content of these programmes. The main purpose will be to ensure that no discharge takes place until the Health Board have formally notified the local authority of their intentions and the local authority have had an opportunity to assess the needs of the individual for social work support services. It will be for the Health Boards and local authorities jointly to satisfy themselves that the combined availability of the relevant community-based health services and social work services will allow the individual concerned to live in the community and that effective arrangements are made as to how these needs are met. In particular a named individual should be appointed to ensure the needs are met.

10.28 The availability of specialist social work support services for people with mental illness is of crucial importance in making community care a reality for this vulnerable group. The Government recognises that there is increasing professionalism within authorities, particularly through mental health officers and hospital social workers, to provide care and support both to former long-stay patients and to out-patients whose health needs may still require periodic hospitalisation. This professionalism is not, however, always matched by community facilities to supplement care programmes.

10.29 The Government has decided therefore to introduce a specific grant to local authorities to help accelerate the development of community-based services for people with mental illness. This grant will be project based and subject to review after a fixed period. It will be designed to increase the facilities in the community both to prevent unnecessary hospital admissions and to provide for patients discharged to live in the community. The Government considers that it is important in the case of mental illness to have a wide range of services available in the community and to make full use of the resourses which the voluntary sector have to offer in this field. The form and implementation of the grant will be the subject of consultation with local authorities.

Resources

10.30 The growth of expenditure on community care in Great Britain as a whole is described in the first part of Chapter 8. The Government's proposals for funding residential and nursing home care as set out in that chapter and the proposals for preserved rights of existing claimants in Chapter 9 apply fully to Scotland. These changes will see local authorities assuming responsibility for an increasing number of persons needing support. Detailed arrangements for the transfer of resources, which will be phased appropriately, will be settled in the Public Expenditure Survey following discussions with local authority interests in Scotland.

Conclusion

10.31 The Government's proposals are designed to help people with special needs to lead as full and independent a life as possible in the community for as long as they wish to do so. Under these proposals resources will be better targeted to develop the range of services required. Demographic and other pressures will make it increasingly important to secure the best balance between the different types of health and social care. The public sector agencies will continue to play their part as providers but there will be a major role for the private sector and voluntary organisations in securing better, more flexible services with a broader choice for individuals, more closely matched to their needs.

CHAPTER ELEVEN: COMMUNITY CARE IN WALES

CHAPTER ELEVEN: COMMUNITY CARE IN WALES

A New Framework For Development

11.1 The past 10 years have seen remarkable development and growth in health and personal social services in Wales, particularly for the most vulnerable in society, including elderly people, those with physical disabilities or mental handicaps and those suffering from a mental illness. The proposals in this White Paper for an improved framework for the delivery of community care will provide still greater opportunities for such people in Wales to maintain their independence as valued members of their communities.

11.2 As elsewhere in Great Britain, up to now those in Wales who need help with social care, beyond what families and friends provide, have had to look primarily to two separate sources: to the social services authorities for home care, day care and some residential care, supplemented often to a significant extent by family practitioner and community health services; but to social security offices for payments towards the costs of places in private and voluntary residential care and nursing homes. This has not enabled the public agencies to secure the best packages of care for all individuals, although many have undoubtedly benefited from residential and nursing home care. This has worked against the generally accepted objective of securing that people should be able to live independent and fulfilled lives in their own homes and communities, wherever possible and where they so wish, with residential or nursing home care being a positive choice where that, rather than domiciliary care, best meets individuals' needs and wishes.

11.3 Against this background, the proposals in this White Paper regarding changes to the arrangements for social security; the respective roles of the social services and health authorities;the crucial part to be played by general practitioners and the voluntary and private sectors; the new arrangements for the inspection of residential care; the proposals regarding assessments of those in need of social or nursing care; and the arrangements for charging for services, which are described in earlier chapters, apply equally to Wales. There are, however, distinctive needs and circumstances in Wales which require special arrangements for the planning and development of services and to secure quality assurance in service delivery. These are described in the rest of this Chapter.

A Record Of Achievement

Elderly People

11.4 The numbers in need of care and support in Wales are substantial. The longer people live, the more care and support they are likely to require. Since 1979 the number of people aged over 65 has grown by 39,000 to 471,000, or 1 in 6 of the population. All of this rise is accounted for by those over 75 whose number grew between 1979 and 1988 by 40,000 to 199,000, an increase of 25%, and the number over 85 rose from under 29,000 to nearly 41,000, an increase of over 42%. A number of studies suggest that the difficulties of maintaining a dependent elderly person in the community are greater for those suffering from mental incapacity. Approximately 10% of people aged 65 and over and 25% of those over 80 show evidence of intellectual failure. Physical disability is also a problem facing many elderly people. From major surveys of those with disabilities carried out by the OPCS in 1985 and 1986, it has been estimated that 58,000 of those aged 65 or over who have disabilities would rank 7 to 10 on a disability score of 1 to 10.

11.5 Service provision for elderly people has expanded significantly over the past decade. Expenditure on the NHS in Wales has grown by approaching 45% in real terms since 1978/79 and made possible record levels of patient care from which elderly people in particular have benefited. For instance, between 1979 and 1987 the district nurse and health visitor service increased by 32% its contacts with elderly people; the number of chiropodists employed in the NHS increased by 54%; hip replacement operations increased by 50%; operations for the removal of cataracts more than doubled; and knee replacement operations more than trebled.

11.6 There has also been major development in personal social services, made possible by an increase in net expenditure in real terms since 1978/79 of 40%. There has been, for instance, since 1980 a 74% increase in provision of adaptations and personal aids to people of 65 and over, and a 40% increase in the number of home helps.

11.7 Most elderly people live in their own homes and an increasing number own them. In 1986 it was estimated that 64% lived in owner-occupied dwellings and some 150,000, almost 30%, lived alone. They, amongst others, are benefiting directly from the Government's programme of home improvement and adaptation in Wales. Over the last decade public expenditure on renovation and adaptations to homes owned either privately or by local authorities has exceeded £1 billion. Between the Welsh House Condition Survey conducted in 1981 and the survey in 1986 there was a reduction of almost half in the proportion of homes lacking an amenity, together with a significant reduction in the overall rate of unfitness. Notwithstanding this massive investment, in 1986 32,000 households headed by a pensioner lived in a dwelling classified as unfit and an additional 8,000 households lived in fit dwellings which lacked one or more basic amenity. Compared with all households these "pensioner" households were more poorly housed - 13% lived in these categories of substandard dwellings compared with 9% of all households.

11.8 Accordingly, housing providers are now being encouraged to feature clear strategies for elderly people and for those with special needs in their performance and planning documents. The Government's proposals for the introduction of a new scheme for renovation grants will lead to a greater proportion of local authority support for home improvements benefiting elderly people. This activity will also build on the unprecedented expansion of recent years of housing built specifically for elderly people. 'Care and repair' agency services and 'stay put' schemes will continue to play a valuable supplementary role in improving the standards of accommodation for elderly people in their own homes.

11.9 In addition to these programmes, the Welsh Office has provided substantial funding under the initiative for the elderly to stimulate new developments in the delivery of care in a more flexible, co-ordinated and cost-effective way. Some 30 projects are now being funded for up to 5 years at a total cost of over £6.25 million.

Physical Disability

11.10 Based on the OPCS surveys, on a scale of 1 to 10 covering physical and mental disability, 90,000 adults and 9,000 children in Wales scored 7 or more. Over 80% of these live in their own homes as do 95% of all those with disabilities.

11.11 Fully an estimated 64% of those with severe disabilities are over 65, and the expansion of services for elderly people has already been described. Services have grown too for younger people with physical handicaps. For instance, the annual provision of personal aids for this younger group has increased by more than 75% since 1980.

Mental Illness

11.12 It is not possible to say categorically how many people in Wales are suffering from a mental illness or its effects. But it has been estimated that as many as 200,000, or 1 in 14 of the total population, have suffered or will suffer from a serious mental illness at some time in their lives. Since the early 1970s the number of in-patients in designated mental illness hospital beds has fallen from over 6,000 to under 4,000, with an 11% reduction since 1980. Admissions, however, rose by 16% between 1977 and 1987 to over 13,000. Over the past decade there has been a significant expansion too in out-patient services, in day care and in community health services. This development has been assisted by annually recurrent special investment by the Welsh Office totalling more than £13 million in 1989/90. A full analysis of service provision is given in Chapter 2 and Annex 2 of "Mental Illness: A Strategy for Wales" published in June this year.

Mental Handicap

11.13 It is estimated that about 10,000 people in Wales have severe mental handicaps. The all-Wales mental handicap strategy has made possible over the past 6½ years an unprecedented expansion of community services, which in turn has made possible a reduction in the number of people cared for in mental handicap hospitals and other long-term institutional care. The number of people receiving support in their own homes has risen from just 41 in 1982/83 to 2,110 in 1988/89; the number of places enabling adults with a mental handicap to live in their own ordinary housing from 166 to 696; the number of places in short-term care in domestic settings from 34 to 549; the number of children being cared for in family settings from 24 to 81; and the number of people receiving new community-based day services from 37 to 1,107.

11.14 The number of mental handicap hospital in-patients has fallen from 2,089 in 1983 to an estimated 1,555 in 1989. Within these totals, the fall in the number of children under 16 has been even more dramatic, from 72 in 1983 to 6 in 1989. The total number of admissions has been falling too.

11.15 Welsh Office specific grant in support of these new patterns of services has increased to over £18.6 million in 1989/90, an increase of nearly £5 million over provision in 1988/89. On top of this, health and social services authorities spent some £4.2 million extra in real terms in 1987/88 compared with 1982/83 and had redeployed £3.3 million from the old to the new patterns of services.

Other Achievements

11.16 The voluntary sector too has expanded its contribution to care significantly, and this has been assisted by a rise in the Welsh Office's special support. For instance, since 1985/86 the level of grant for community care projects, over and above those under the urban programme and the mental handicap strategy, has increased in real terms by over 42%.

11.17 In addition, an estimated £65 million was spent in Wales in 1988/89 on social security benefits to help meet the costs of those cared for in private and voluntary sector residential care and nursing homes compared with £0.6 million in 1979/80. Between 1979 and 1988 the number of private and voluntary sector residential care homes in Wales went up from 92 to 457, and the number of places increased fourfold to over 7,800. There were 42 private and voluntary sector nursing homes in Wales in 1982; by 1987 the number was 167 and the number of beds had again increased more than four-fold, to over 4,000. Most of these increases have been in provision for elderly people.

11.18 Notwithstanding this massive expansion of public expenditure to improve care and support, the greater part of care for most people at most times of their lives continues to be provided by their families and friends. Based on the 1985 Informal Carers Survey by OPCS it is estimated that some 290,000 people in Wales care in private households for disabled or infirm relatives, friends or neighbours. Approximately 60% of carers are women.

Demographic Change And The Challenge For Caring

11.19 Over the next 20 years the number of people over 75 in Wales is expected to increase by 48,000, or 25% and the very elderly - those over 85 - by 26,4000, an increase of 65%. Most old people lead fulfilled and independent lives. Nonetheless, there will, as a result of this demographic change, be more people in the population with physical disabilities and with mental illnesses associated with old age. The numbers suffering from other mental illnesses and with mental handicaps are, however, unlikely to change significantly.

11.20 At the same time that numbers in need of care will rise, the number of people in the 45 to 65 age group, which provides a substantial proportion of informal care, are expected to increase by only 19% over the next two decades. Moreover, wider social and economic developments such as the increased mobility of labour, the growing number of women at work, the increasing number of single-parent families, and increased rates of separation and divorce, are all likely to reduce the number of people who can devote significant amounts of time to the care and support of their frail elderly or other disabled relatives. Although these changes have to be kept in perspective - they represent developments in the need for care and a decline in the availability of informal care at the margin of the existing pattern - it is nonetheless an important margin which will represent a major challenge for health and social care.

Planning For Care

·Mental Illness and Mental Handicap

11.21 In the past, services in Wales for people with mental illnesses or mental handicaps have been imbalanced and poorly distributed across Wales. People have often had to travel too far to receive care, and the choice has too often been between care in isolated institutions or of little or no support in people's own homes and communities. Faced with this flawed inheritance, and the need for a major re-shaping of patterns of services and the underlying distribution of resources, the Welsh Office has provided a framework for health and social services authorities, the voluntary and private sectors, other agencies and representatives of users of services, to work together to develop new, more decentralised patterns of services.

11.22 The Welsh Office has issued guidance on the form and content of joint plans, including the specification of essential core services, to promote the development of mental handicap services. The plans provide the basis for the systematic annual review of performance and the setting of agreed targets for service development. These arrangements will continue. An improved data base is being developed by the Welsh Office, in co-operation with the health and social services authorities, to provide for core information in plans and to facilitate a common framework for monitoring and evaluation. It is proposed to introduce this next year.

11.23 There will be a full review of service development and of the framework provided by the strategy in 1991/92, in consultation with all relevant interests, so that decisions can be announced in good time before the end of the strategy's initially programmed 10 years at the end of 1992/93. It remains the Welsh Office's intention to transfer to the county councils, through the arrangements for revenue support grant, the resources made available to them by means of specific grant under the strategy, as soon as it is satisfied that the new patterns of services are sufficiently well developed.

11.24 From 1990/91 all development in mental illness services will take place within the framework of the all-Wales strategy which was launched in June this year. In accordance with guidance issued by the Welsh Office, joint plans are currently being prepared by health and social services authorities, working together with all other relevant interests. These arrangements will continue. An agreed data set to provide core information for future plans, and to provide the basis for the strategic monitoring and evaluation of services, is being developed with the health and social services authorities. It is proposed to introduce this next year. Guidance on the arrangements for systematic annual review and for the setting of targets for service development, on the basis of the joint plans, will be issued early in 1990.

Other Groups, including Elderly People and those with Physical Disabilities

11.25 Services for elderly people and for those with physical disabilities, including people suffering from chronic illness, are not, as is the case with mental illness and mental handicap services, dominated by an inheritance of large, relatively isolated institutions. Nonetheless, there is a need to ensure that the significant public investment in service provision for these groups is properly planned and sensitively targeted in response to the greatest needs, with an emphasis on maximising each individual's independence. A crucial part of that process, over a period of years, will involve changing the balance of care away from residential care and nursing homes towards domiciliary care, whilst at the same time ensuring that those who need residential or nursing home care continue to have access to it.

Social Care Plans

11.26 To provide the basis for service development and delivery, it is proposed that social care plans should be prepared and published by the social services authorities in Wales. These plans will be expected to bring together the contributions of social services authorities, health authorities, family practitioner services, the voluntary and private sectors, housing authorities and housing associations, and to take into account the views of the users of services, to secure the best use of the total resources available for care.

11.27 Plans will need to include clear statements about the philosophy and aims of services; an analysis of current provision in relation to needs; clear statements of priority for service provision and development, within available resources; the agreed local arrangements for the assessment of individuals' care needs; and arrangements for monitoring and evaluation. They will be expected to cover domiciliary and day services, community living schemes in ordinary housing, residential and nursing home care, relevant continuing care in hospitals, and the roles of particular agencies and service providers, including the private and voluntary sectors. They will need to show the way in which services will work in support of networks of informal care. Plans will be expected to provide an over-view of service provision across all client groups, with the aim of ensuring equal access to services in relation to need, regardless of client group labels.

11.28 As regards housing, social care plans should take account of the progressive development of housing investment programmes, which have given significantly greater priority to special needs and to the provision of homes that can be flexibly adapted to enable people to live independently for as long as they wish. It will be essential that social services departments and housing providers maintain close liaison over the development of these plans. It is equally important that housing providers give sustained and positive attention to the housing requirements of special needs and community care. Housing for Wales will provide the strategic thrust to enable the housing associations to maximise their contribution.

11.29 No changes are proposed in the roles and responsibilities of housing authorities and associations in respect of special needs and community care. District housing authorities will, therefore, be expected to play their full part in facilitating strategic development at the local level, in partnership with housing associations and with the voluntary and private sectors. The Welsh Office will provide advice on how best to feature development objectives in the field of community care in providers' existing strategic planning documents.

11.30 It is intended that the social care plans should be concise and action-orientated. It is proposed that they should be prepared with reference to an agreed core data set, to be produced jointly by the Welsh Office with relevant interests, building on the work already being done in the fields of mental illness and mental handicap, to provide the basis for strategic monitoring. They will have to be submitted to the Welsh Office. Detailed guidance on the form and broad content of plans, including their relationship to the existing joint plans for mental handicap and mental illness services, will be issued in the Spring of 1990, following consultation with social services and health authorities and other interests.

11.31 The guidance will, in respect of elderly people, take into account the results of the continuous appraisal of Welsh Office grant aided projects under the initiative on the care of the elderly.

11.32 The Welsh Office will shortly be issuing advice on good practice in the care of those with physical and sensory disabilities. That advice will be taken into account in the guidance to be issued on the preparation of social care plans. In the longer term, the results of two current surveys on services provided for disabled people by the NHS, and by local authorities and the voluntary sector, will supplement this guidance.

11.33 The first plans will need to be published before April 1991 to provide the local framework for authorities to fulfil from that time their wider responsibilities as proposed in Chapter 3.

The Funding Of Services

11.34 It is proposed that the social services authorities should have the responsibility and the budget for social care. District health authorities and family practitioners services authorities will continue to have responsibility and the budgets to ensure the provision of health care for those who need it.

11.35 Government financial support for social services authorities will be principally by means of revenue support grant. Resources will be transferred to the local authorities from the social security programme progressively from 1 April 1991, taking into account the continued eligibility for financial help under the existing benefit arrangements of those already in registered residential and nursing home care before the new arrangements come into effect. Decisions on resource issues will be taken in next year's Public Expenditure Survey following discussions with the local authorities and other key interests in Wales about the implications of the proposals aimed to ensure their successful introduction.

11.36 The Government will continue to make resources available to assist in creating the conditions in which housing providers can help to support effective social care, and to achieve value for money.

11.37 The investment of specific grant-aid by the Welsh Office in support of the all-Wales mental handicap and mental illness strategies will continue where plans demonstrate the best possible use of the total resources available for care. They must, therefore, include proposals for the progressive redeployment of the existing resources on new patterns of service development in line with the strategies, and demonstrate that specific central funding is essential to enable the new patterns of services to come about.

11.38 The Welsh Office proposes to bring together and target existing grant-aid under the initiative on the care of the elderly, and that for elderly people and other groups, including those with physical disabilities, which has hitherto been made available under the Urban Programme. The aim will be to stimulate the development of flexible community care arrangements, with an emphasis on the enhancement of cost-effective domiciliary care. Decisions on financial support will take into account the adequacy of relevant elements of the social care plans of the authorities seeking financial assistance.

11.39 These arrangements will come fully into effect for developments starting in 1991/92. For 1990/91 applications may still be made under the initiative on the care of the elderly, but priority will be given to schemes which aim to fulfil White Paper objectives. Detailed guidance on schemes starting in 1990/91 has been issued. Applications for schemes starting in 1990/91 under the Urban Programme have already been made and will be considered in the normal way.

11.40 In the light of these new arrangements, the Welsh Office will, after the current year (1989/90), no longer make available earmarked funds via the health authorities for the development of social care under the arrangements known as joint finance. Health authorities will, however, still be able to make payments for the development of social care within the existing legislative framework, and they are encouraged to do so where this would lead to the best use of the total resources available for care.

11.41 The Welsh Office set out proposals to promote the more effective management and delivery of community health and related social care services in Circular WHC(89)23 on the follow-up to the report of the Review of Community Nursing Services in Wales. This encouraged, in particular, the establishment of Primary Care Liaison Committees to bring together in joint working arrangements the key staffs of family practitioner, community health and personal social services. The Welsh Office is making available over £100,000 to support this approach in 1989/90. Funding will be available for at least the next three years.

Quality Assurance

11.42 The maintenance of quality in the provision of services properly falls to the agencies which have the responsibility for planning and securing those services, namely social services authorities in the case of social care, district health authorities in the case of community health services and family practitioner committees in respect of the services provided by general practitioners. The Welsh Office has recently launched consultation with the aim of publishing, before the end of this year, an agreed strategy for quality assurance throughout the National Health Service in the Principality. In respect of personal social services, county councils will enjoy, through responsibility for publicly provided resources for social care, significantly enhanced leverage to assure quality. The proposals in Chapter 5 for the establishment of new inspection and registration units within each county council will act in a complementary way to ensure consistency of approach to quality assurance as between directly provided services of the social services authority and those provided by the private and voluntary sectors.

11.43 Notwithstanding this central role of the social services and health authorities, there is a well-accepted need for vulnerable groups to enjoy the additional protection of independent mechanisms of quality assurance. It is therefore proposed that the present Social Work Service (SWS) of the Welsh Office will be renamed the Social Services Inspectorate (SSI) to reflect the strengthening of commitment to these processes. The Social Services Inspectorate will continue, under existing statutory powers of the Secretary of State, to inspect personal social services. It is also proposed that it should play an important part in the Welsh Office's appraisal of authorities' social care plans. In addition, it is proposed that the SSI should advise and monitor the operation of the new registration and inspection units of the local authorities.

11.44 The All-Wales Advisory Panel on Services for People with Mental Handicaps has produced proposals for strengthening the independent review of services. The Secretary of State has published the proposals for consultation. These will be taken forward as part of a wider consideration of the arrangements for the independent review of all community care services in Wales, taking into account the current England and Wales review of the Health Advisory Service (HAS). The HAS carries out an important review role in respect of services for elderly people and those with mental illnesses.

Enabling Staff to Meet the Challenge

11.45 Social services authorities will need to give careful consideration to the training and development of management, planning and front-line staffs to fulfil the roles outlined in this White Paper. For many front-line staff joint training with those working in family practitioner services, community health services and housing can be expected to play an important part, particularly in developing common understanding and joint working arrangements for case management and assessment.

11.46 The SSI intends to build on the established Management Development Project which involves all social services authorities in the Principality. The project, designed to strengthen management and provide better targeted objectives for service development and the evaluation of outcomes for those who receive care, will be developed to help the personal social services maximise the opportunities to improve care provided by the Government's proposals. The SSI will also work with the local authorities to establish an improved data base of manpower and training resources to help ensure a skilled workforce to fulfil the objectives of the White Paper.

Table 1

Gross Expenditure on Core Services for Community Care

All figures in millions for Great Britain

	79/80 £m	87/88 £m		79/80 £m	87/88 £m
LA Domiciliary Care			**LA Residential Care**		
Home Helps	209	535	Elderly	458	914
Meals on Wheels	27	59	YPH	30	44
Aids and Adaptations	15	49	MH Children	16	52
Day Care for Elderly	27	77	MH Adults	44	144
.... for YPH, MI, MH	35	78	Mental Illness	12	29
Adult Training	63	167			
Social Work	88	202			
LA Domiciliary Care	464	1,167	**LA Residential Care**	560	1,183
Community Health			**Income Support**		
*District Nursing	109	261	For Residential and		
*Health Visiting	7	15	Nursing Home Care	10	774
Chiropody	19	44			
Community Health	135	320	**Income Support**	10	774
Total Domiciliary	599	1,487	**Total Residential**	570	1,957
Total Community Care	1,169	3,444			

NB: Administration costs, joint finance and the community care element of some social security benefits have been excluded. In particular expenditure on Attendance Allowance and Invalid Care Allowance has risen from 205m in 1979/80 to 1,081 in 1987/88 - a real terms increase of 200%.

It has been assumed that only 45% of social work, 70% of district nursing and 8% of health visiting expenditure is appropriate to community care for these client groups. It has been also assumed that all of this is for people in non-residential settings.

* Welsh figures for 1979/80 are estimated.

Chart 1

Expenditure on Community Care by Agency

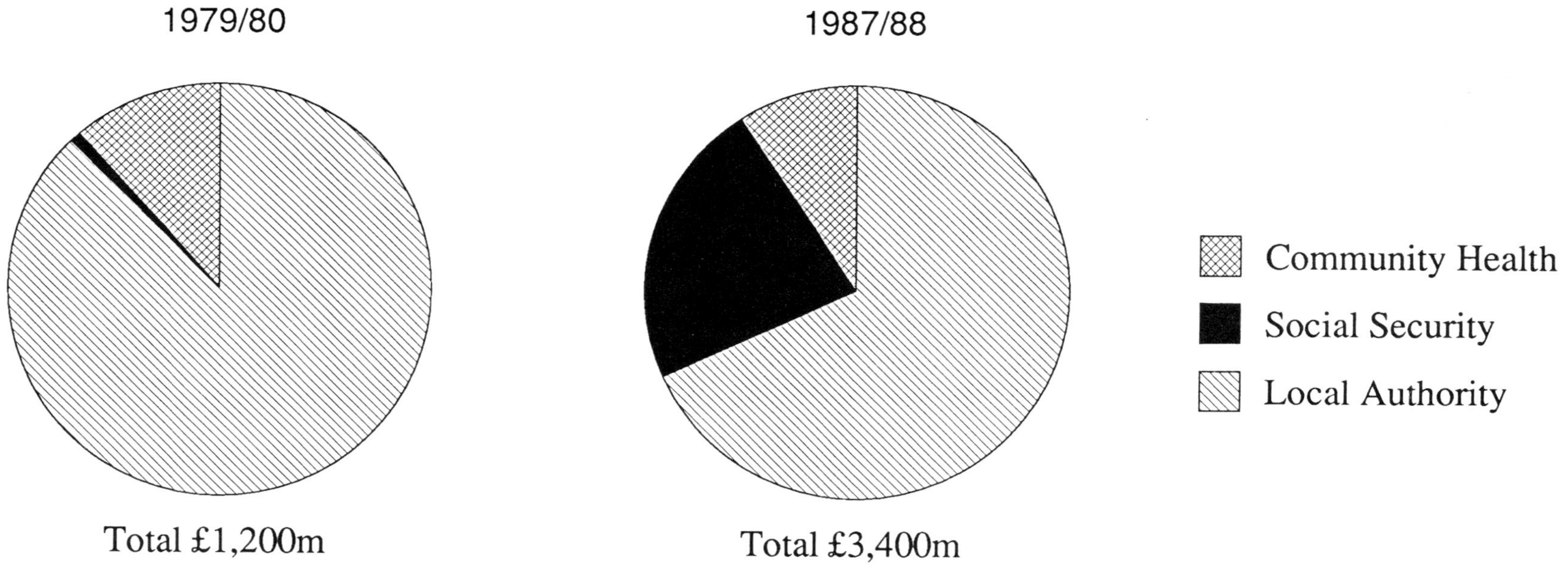

Note: Chart shows gross expenditure for Great Britain in cash terms covering core services as detailed in Table 1.

Chart 2

Expenditure on Residential and Domiciliary Services by Agency

GB 1988/89 Prices

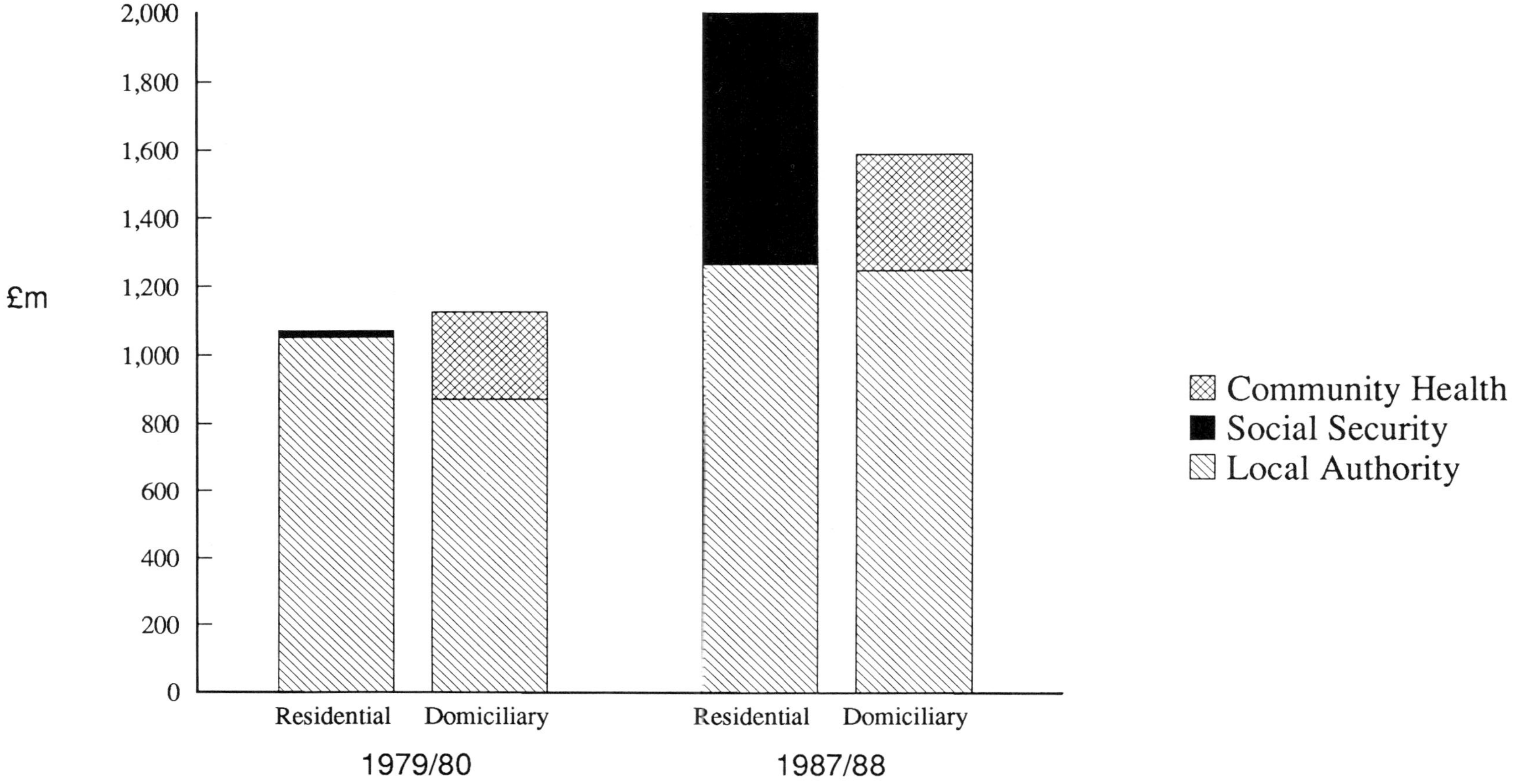

Note: Chart shows gross expenditure for Great Britain in real terms in 1988/89 prices. Only core services covered as in Table 1.

Chart 3

Income Support Expenditure on Residential Care Homes and Nursing Homes

GB 1988/89 Prices

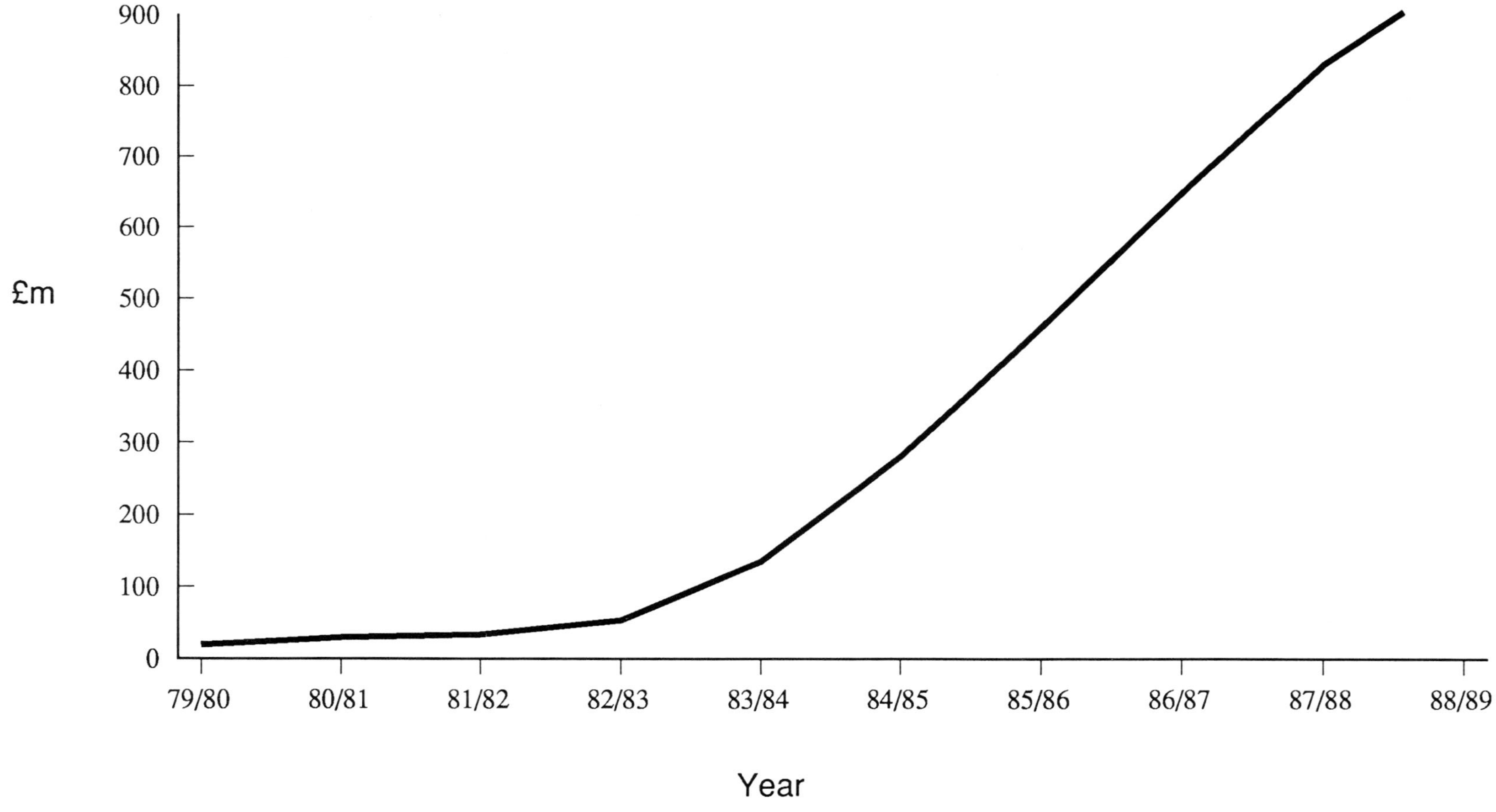

Chart 4

Projected Population for Great Britain by Age

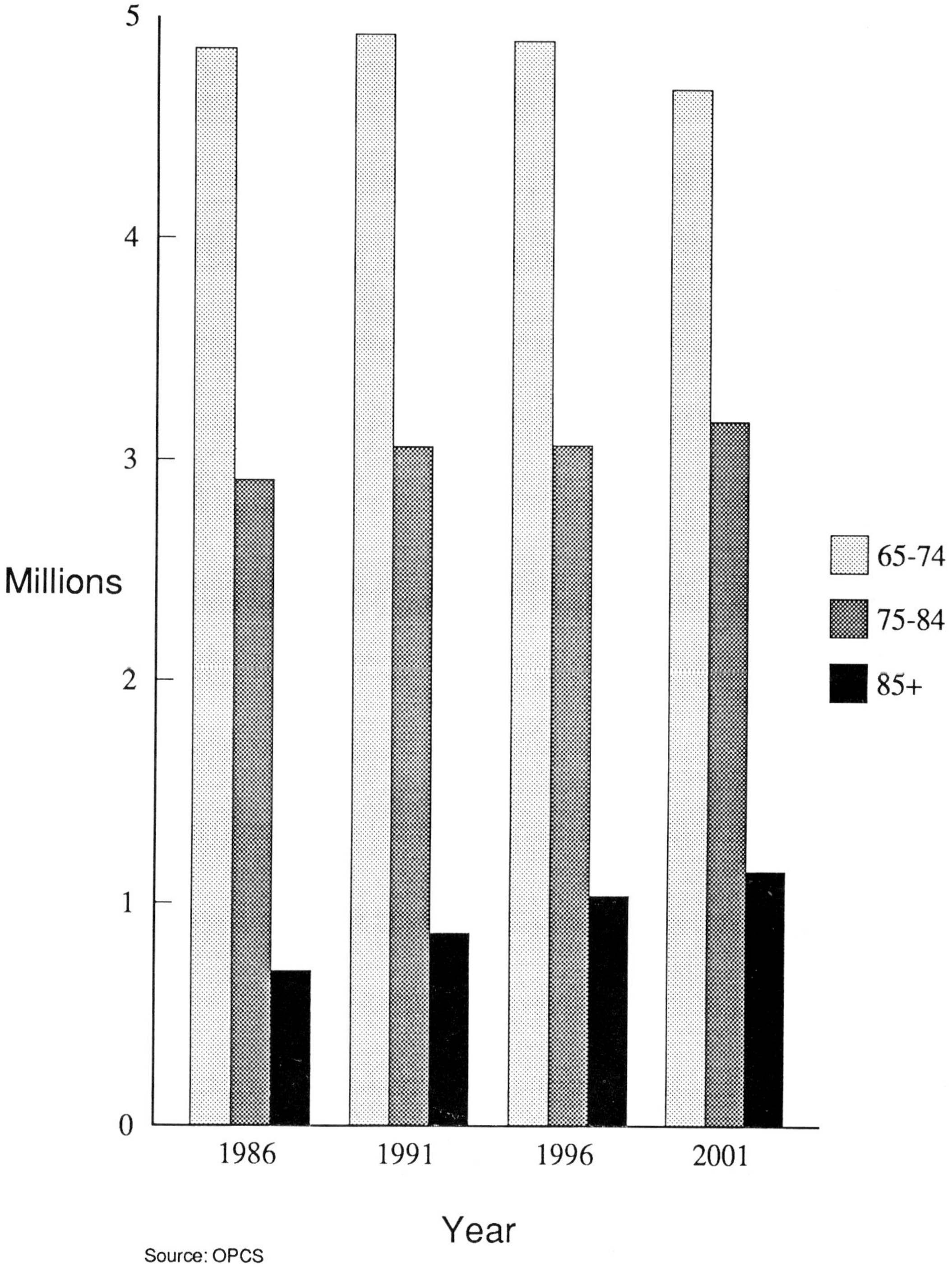

Source: OPCS

Chart 5

Projected Numbers of Disabled Elderly

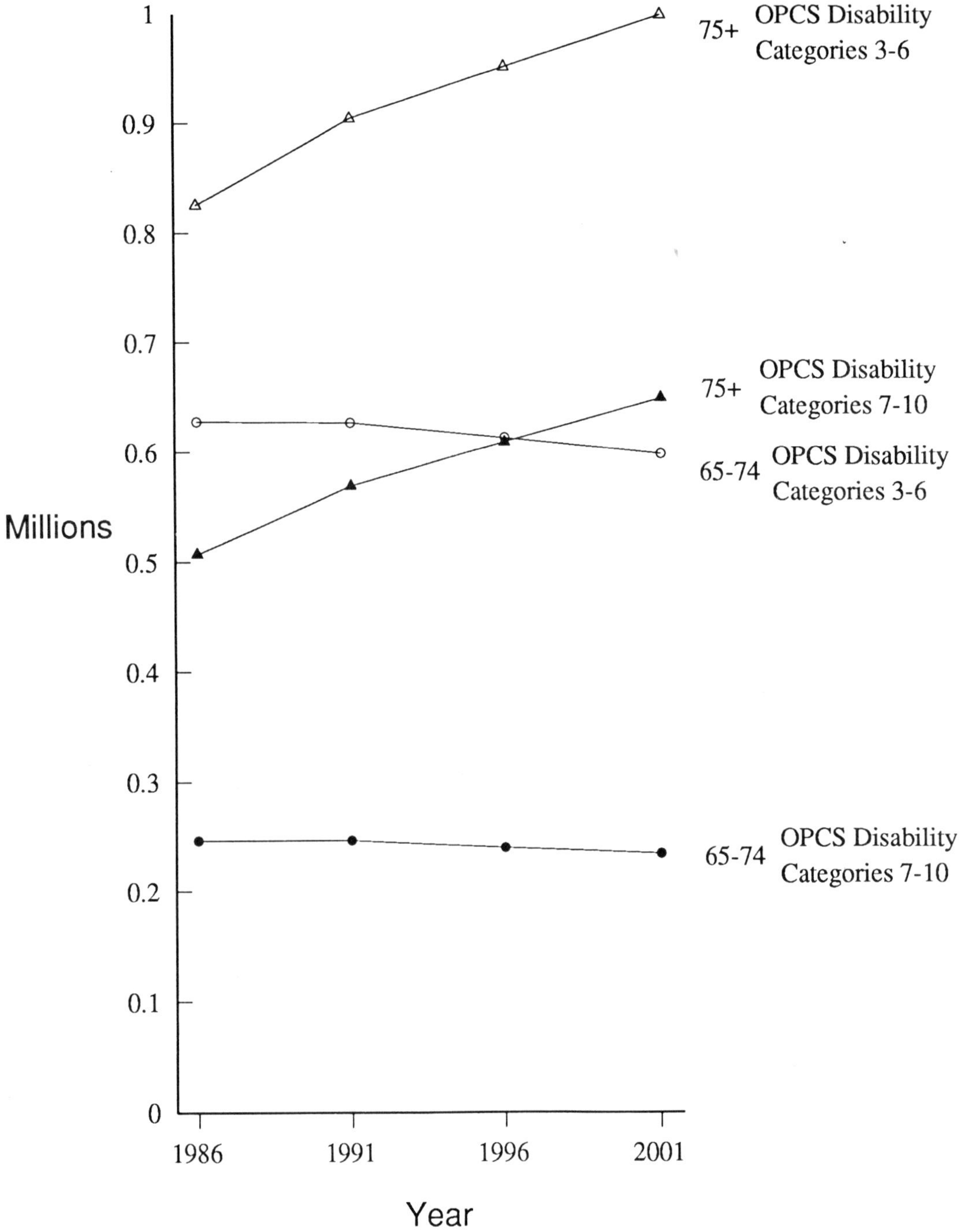

Note: Source OPCS Disability Survey. For the purpose of the survey, OPCS ranked the severity of disability from 1-10, where 10 is the most severe.

Chart 6

Estimated Cumulative Rate of Transfer of DSS Care Expenditure

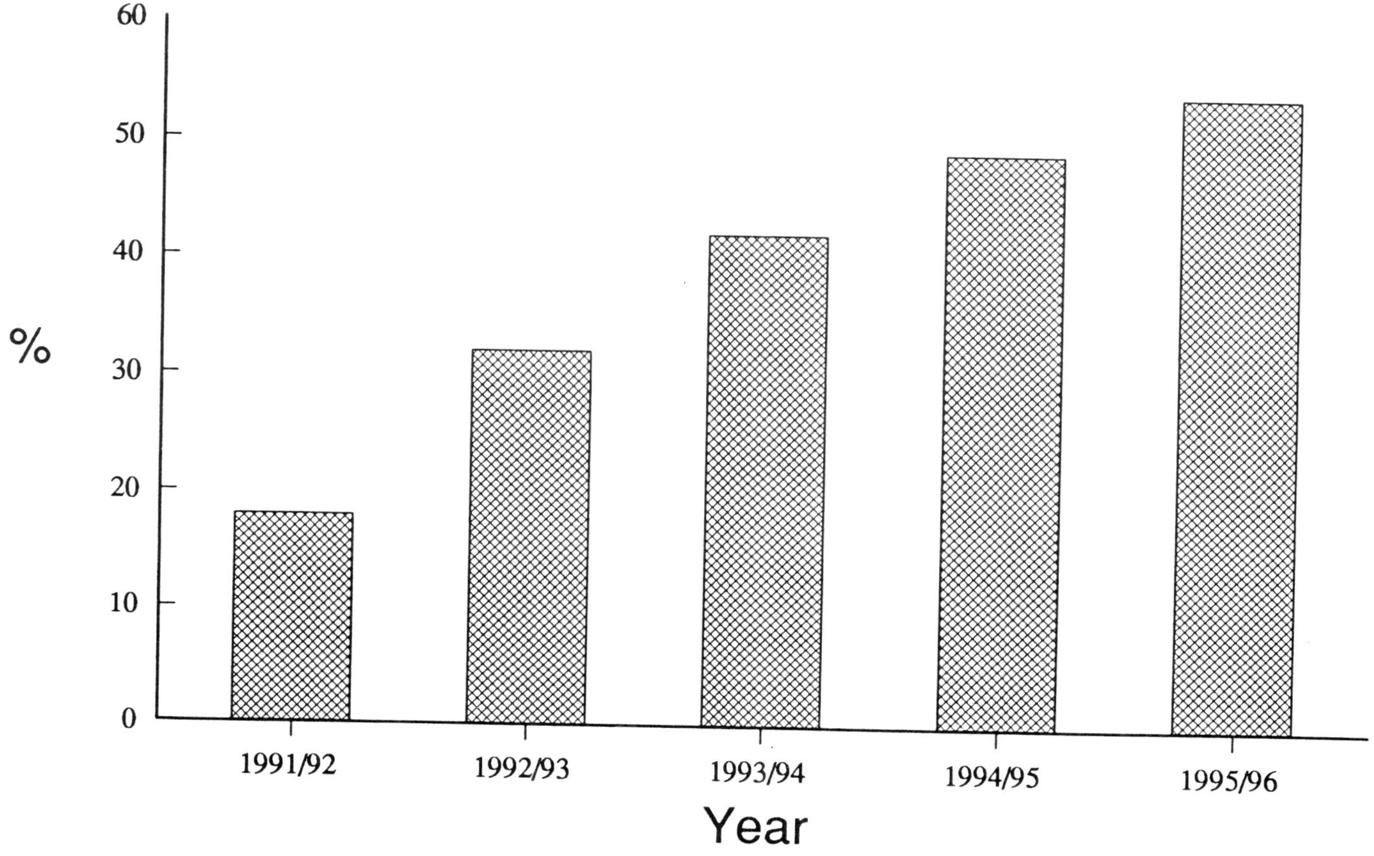

Note: Chart shows cumulative share of total transferred by year.

Chart 7

Community Care - Flow of Resources

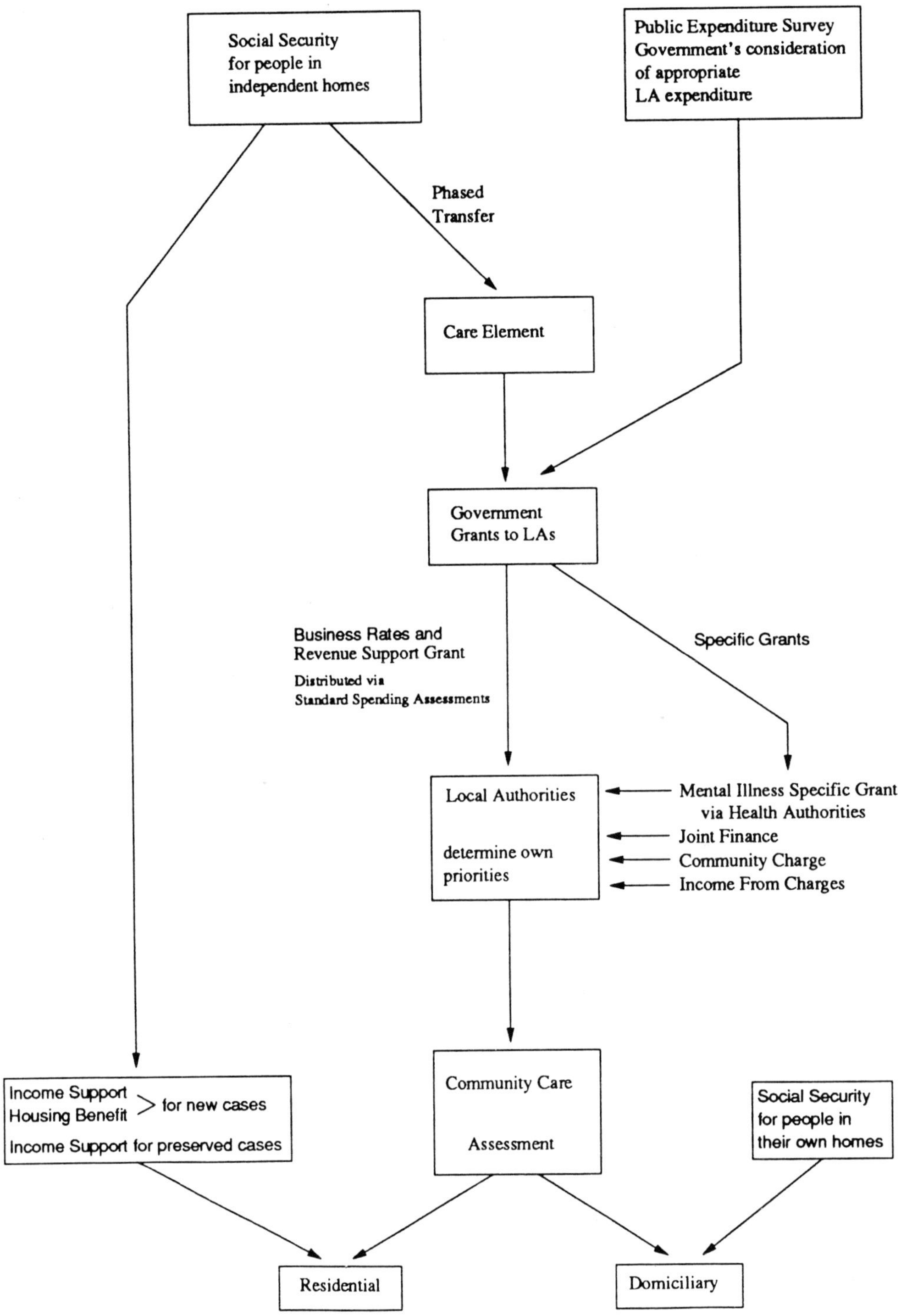

Printed in the United Kingdom for HMSO
Dd 0509094 7/92 C50 514048 Ord 203661 40/22142